Why Johnny Can't Read ∽ *AND WHAT*

YOU CAN DO ABOUT IT

by Rudolf Flesch

HARPER & BROTHERS, PUBLISHERS

New York

Library of Congress catalog card number: 55-6577

c.2

To Stephen

Contents

Preface

This double-purpose book, with its rather awkward double-purpose title, needs a bit of explanation. Let me put it this way: Just as war is "too serious a matter to be left to the generals," so, I think, the teaching of reading is too important to be left to the educators. This book, therefore, is not addressed to teachers and teachers' college professors but to fathers and mothers. I tried, to the best of my ability, to write a book they can use to help their children read.

But in the United States of 1955, a simple "home primer" wouldn't have a chance. It would have to make its way against the almost solid opposition of teachers, school officials, and educational "experts." And that's why this book is not only a practical handbook but also a little compendium of arguments against our current system of teaching reading.

So please forgive me if the structure of the book seems a little peculiar. Most of the first part is theory and argument, and all of the second part is straight "home primer." But there is also some practical stuff in Chapters 2 and 10, which I felt had to go in there because otherwise the rest of the book wouldn't be fully intelligible.

Perhaps some readers will have no use for the exercises; perhaps some others will want to have the book for the exercises only. I can't tell. At any rate, the exercises can be used independently by following the instructions on pp. 139-140.

R. F.

Why Johnny Can't Read

Chapter I

A LETTER TO JOHNNY'S MOTHER

Dear Mary:

I have decided to start this book with a letter to you. You know that the idea came to me when I offered to help Johnny with his reading. It's really his book—or yours. So the only proper way to start it is with the words "Dear Mary."

You remember when I began to work with Johnny half a year ago. That was when he was twelve and they put him back into sixth grade because he was unable to read and couldn't possibly keep up with the work in junior high. So I told you that I knew of a way to teach reading that was altogether different from what they do in schools or in remedial reading courses or anywhere else. Well, you trusted me, and you know what has happened since. Today Johnny can read—not perfectly, to be sure, but anyone can see that in a few more months he will have caught up with other boys of his age. And he is happy again: You and I and everyone else can see that he is a changed person.

I think Johnny will go to college. He has a very good mind, as you know, and I don't see why he shouldn't become a doctor or a lawyer or an engineer. There is a lot in Johnny that has never come to the surface because of this reading trouble.

Since I started to work with Johnny, I have looked into this whole reading business. I worked my way through a mountain of books and articles on the subject, I talked to dozens of people, and I spent many hours in classrooms, watching what was going on.

What I found is absolutely fantastic. The teaching of reading —all over the United States, in all the schools, in all the text-books—is totally wrong and flies in the face of all logic and common sense. Johnny couldn't read until half a year ago for the simple reason that nobody ever showed him how. Johnny's only problem was that he was unfortunately exposed to an ordinary American school.

You know that I was born and raised in Austria. Do you know that there are no remedial reading cases in Austrian schools? Do you know that there are no remedial reading cases in Germany, in France, in Italy, in Norway, in Spain—practically anywhere in the world except in the United States? Do you know that there was no such thing as remedial reading in this country either until about thirty years ago? Do you know that the teaching of reading never was a problem anywhere in the world until the United States switched to the present method around about 1925?

This sounds incredible, but it is true. One of the articles on reading that I found was by a Dr. Ralph C. Preston, of the University of Pennsylvania, who reported on his ex-periences on a trip through Western Germany in the April, 1953, *Elementary School Journal*. Dr. Preston visited a number of classrooms in Hamburg and Munich. "After the experience of hearing these German children read aloud," he says, "I began to attach some credence to a generally expressed opinion of German teachers that before the end of Grade 2 almost any child can read orally (without regard to degree of comprehen-sion) almost anything in print!"

Of course, Dr. Preston, being an American educator, didn't draw the obvious conclusion from what he saw. The explana-tion is simply that the method used over there works, and the method used in our schools does not. We too could have perfect readers in all schools at the end of second grade if we taught our children by the system used in Germany.

Now, what is this system? It's very simple. Reading means

getting meaning from certain combinations of letters. Teach the child what each letter stands for and he can read.

Ah no, you say, it can't be that simple. But it is. Let me give you an illustration.

I don't know whether you know any shorthand. Let's suppose you don't. Let's suppose you decide to learn how to read English shorthand.

Right away you say that nobody learns how to *read* shorthand. People who want to know shorthand learn how to *write* it; the reading of it comes by the way.

Exactly. That's why shorthand is such a good illustration of this whole thing. It's just a system of getting words on paper. Ordinary writing is another such system. Morse code is a third. Braille is a fourth. And so it goes. There are all sorts of systems of translating spoken words into a series of symbols so that they can be written down and read back.

Now the way to learn any such system is to learn to write and to read it at the same time. And how do you do that? The obvious answer is, By taking up one symbol after another and learning how to write it and how to recognize it. Once you are through the whole list of symbols, you can read and write; the rest is simply practice—learning to do it more and more automatically.

Since the dawn of time people have learned mechanical means of communication in this way—smoke signals and drums in the jungle and flag language and I don't know what all. You take up one item after another, learn what it stands for, learn how to reproduce it and how to recognize it, and there you are.

Shorthand, as I said, is an excellent example. I don't know any English shorthand myself, but I went to a library and looked up the most widely used manual of the Gregg system, the *Functional Method* by L. A. Leslie. Sure enough, it tells you about the symbols one after the other, starting out with the loop that stands for the long *a* in *ache, make,* and *cake.* After a few lessons, you are supposed to know the shape of all the shorthand "letters," and from there on it's just a matter of practice and picking up speed.

Our system of writing—the alphabet—was invented by the Egyptians and the Phoenicians somewhere around 1500 B.C. Before the invention of the alphabet there was only picture writing—a picture of an ox meant "ox," a picture of a house meant "house," and so on. (The Chinese to this day have a system of writing with symbols that stand for whole words.) As soon as people had an alphabet, the job of reading and writing was tremendously simplified. Before that, you had to have a symbol for every word in the language—10,000, 20,000 or whatever the vocabulary range was. Now, with the alphabet, all you had to learn was the letters. Each letter stood for a certain sound, and that was that. To write a word—any word— all you had to do was break it down into its sounds and put the corresponding letters on paper.

So, ever since 1500 B.C. people all over the world—wherever an alphabetic system of writing was used—learned how to read and write by the simple process of memorizing the sound of each letter in the alphabet. When a schoolboy in ancient Rome learned to read, he didn't learn that the written word *mensa* meant a table, that is, a certain piece of furniture with a flat top and legs. Instead, he began by learning that the letter *m* stands for the sound you make when you put your lips together, that *e* means the sound that comes out when you open your mouth about halfway, that *n* is like *m* but with the lips open and the teeth together, that *s* has a hissing sound, and that *a* means the sound made by opening your mouth wide. Therefore, when he saw the written word *mensa* for the first time, he could read it right off and learn, with a feeling of happy discovery, that this collection of letters meant a table. Not only that, he could also write the word down from dictation without ever having seen it before. And not only *that,* he could do this with practically every word in the language.

This is not miraculous, it's the only natural system of learning how to read. As I said, the ancient Egyptians learned that way, and the Greeks and the Romans, and the French and the Germans, and the Dutch and the Portuguese, and the Turks and the Bulgarians and the Esthonians and the Icelanders and the Abyssinians—every single nation throughout history that used an alphabetic system of writing.

Except, as I said before, twentieth-century Americans—and other nations in so far as they have followed our example. And what do we use instead? Why, the only other possible system of course—the system that was in use before the invention of the alphabet in 1500 B.C. We have decided to forget that we write with letters and learn to read English as if it were Chinese. One word after another after another after another. If we want to read materials with a vocabulary of 10,000 words, then we have to memorize 10,000 words; if we want to go to the 20,000 word range, we have to learn, one by one, 20,000 words; and so on. We have thrown 3,500 years of civilization out the window and have gone back to the Age of Hammurabi.

You don't believe me? I assure you what I am saying is literally true. Go to your school tomorrow morning—or if Johnny has brought home one of his readers, look at it. You will immediately see that all the words in it are learned by endless repetition. Not a sign anywhere that letters correspond to sounds and that words can be worked out by pronouncing the letters. No. The child is told what each word means and then they are mechanically, brutally hammered into his brain. Like this:

"We will look," said Susan.
"Yes, yes," said all the children.
"We will look and find it."
So all the boys and girls looked.
They looked and looked for it.
But they did not find it.

Or this:

> "Quack, quack," said the duck.
> He wanted something.
> He did not want to get out.
> He did not want to go to the farm.
> He did not want to eat.
> He sat and sat and sat.

All the reading books used in all our schools, up through fourth and fifth and sixth grade, are collections of stuff like that. Our children learn the word *sat* by reading over and over again about a duck or a pig or a goat that sat and sat and sat. And so with every word in the language.

Every word in the language! You know what that means? It means that if you teach reading by this system, you can't use ordinary reading matter for practice. Instead, all children for three, four, five, six years have to work their way up through a battery of carefully designed readers, each one containing all the words used in the previous one plus a strictly limited number of new ones, used with the exactly "right" amount of repetition. Our children don't read Andersen's *Fairy Tales* any more or *The Arabian Nights* or Mark Twain or Louisa May Alcott or the Mary Poppins books or the Dr. Doolittle books or *anything* interesting and worth while, *because they can't.* It so happens that the writers of these classic children's books wrote without being aware of our Chinese system of teaching reading. So *Little Women* contains words like *grieving* and *serene,* and *Tom Sawyer* has *ague* and *inwardly,* and Bulfinch's *Age of Fable* has *nymph* and *deity* and *incantations.* If a child that has gone to any of our schools faces the word *nymph* for the first time, he is absolutely helpless because nobody has ever told him how to sound out *n* and *y* and *m* and *ph* and read the word off the page.

So what does he get instead? He gets those series of horrible, stupid, emasculated, pointless, tasteless little readers, the stuff and guff about Dick and Jane or Alice and Jerry visiting the farm and having birthday parties and seeing animals in the zoo and going through dozens and dozens of totally unexciting middle-class, middle-income, middle-I.Q. children's activities that offer opportunities for reading "Look, look" or "Yes, yes" or "Come, come" or "See the funny, funny animal." During the past half year I read a good deal of this material and I don't wish that experience on anyone.

Who writes these books? Let me explain this to you in detail, because there is the nub of the whole problem.

There are one or two dozen textbook houses in America. By far the most lucrative part of their business is the publication of readers for elementary schools. There are millions of dollars of profit in these little books. Naturally, the competition is tremendous. So is the investment; so is the sales effort; so is the effort that goes into writing, editing, and illustrating these books.

Now, with our Chinese word-learning system you can't produce a series of readers by printing nice, interesting collections of stuff children of a certain age might like to read. Oh no. Every single story, every single sentence that goes into these books has to be carefully prepared and carefully checked to make sure that each word is one of the 637 that the poor child is supposed to have memorized up to that point—or if it's the 638th word, that it appears in just the right context for optimum guesswork and is then repeated seventeen times at carefully worked-out intervals.

Naturally, the stupendous and frighteningly idiotic work of concocting this stuff can only be done by tireless teamwork of many educational drudges. But if the textbook house put only the drudges on the title page, that wouldn't look impressive enough to beat the competition. So there has to be a "senior author"—someone with a national reputation who teaches how to teach reading at one of the major universities.

And that's why each and every one of the so-called authorities in this field is tied up with a series of readers based on the Chinese word-learning method. As long as you used that method, you have to buy some $30 worth per child of Dr. So-and-so's readers; as soon as you switch to the common-sense method of teaching the sounds of the letters, you can give them a little primer and then proceed immediately to anything from the *Reader's Digest* to *Treasure Island*.

I have personally met some of the leading authorities in the field of reading. They are all very nice ladies and gentlemen, and obviously sincere and well meaning. But they *are* firmly committed to the application of the word method, and it would be inhuman to expect from them an objective point of view.

Consequently it's utterly impossible to find anyone inside the official family of the educators saying anything even slightly favorable to the natural method of teaching reading. Mention the alphabetic method or phonetics or "phonics" and you immediately arouse derision, furious hostility, or icy silence.

For instance, in the May 1952 *Catholic Educator,* Monsignor Clarence E. Elwell published an article "Reading: The Alphabet and Phonics." Monsignor Elwell is Superintendent of Schools of the Diocese of Cleveland and knows what he is talking about. He says: "In a language based on an alphabetic (that is, phonetic) method of coding the spoken word, the only sensible way to teach how to decode the written symbols is (1) by *teaching the phonetic code,* that is, the alphabet, and (2) the manner of coding—letter by letter, left to right. It is as nonsensical to use a whole word method for beginning reading as it would be to teach the Morse code on a whole word basis. . . . A child who has been taught the code and how to use it . . . gains a confident habit in attacking words. Instead of guessing when he comes to a new word, as he did when taught by the sight word method, he now works through a word and to the surprise of the teachers usually comes up with the right answer. . . . After four years' experiment with the introduction of a strong program of phonics at the very beginning of grade one, the experimenter finds teachers convinced and children apparently happier in their success."

What do you think happened when Monsignor Elwell said publicly that our whole system of teaching reading is nonsense? Absolutely nothing. So far as I know, none of the reading "experts" has paid the slightest attention to the Cleveland experiment.

Or take the case of the late Dr. Leonard Bloomfield, professor of linguistics at Yale. Dr. Bloomfield wasn't just any scholar in the field of language; he was universally recognized as the greatest American linguist of modern times. His masterpiece was a book simply called *Language,* published in 1933.

In the last few pages of that book, Bloomfield dealt with the teaching of English and reading in our schools. "Our schools," he wrote, "are utterly benighted in linguistic matters. . . . Nothing could be more discouraging than to read our 'educationalists'' treatises on methods of teaching children to read. The size of this book does not permit a discussion of their varieties of confusion on this subject."

Several years later, Bloomfield took time out to prepare an alphabetic-phonetic primer, based on strictly scientific principles. It was an excellent piece of work, carefully designed to teach children quickly and painlessly. After Bloomfield's death in 1949 his literary executor offered the manuscript to every single elementary textbook publisher in the United States. Not one of them considered it. As I am writing, the book is still unpublished.

The introduction to this Bloomfield primer was, however, published as an article in the *Elementary English Review* in April and May, 1942. I ran across that article eight or ten years ago and that's what started me on this whole business. Taking the ideas of that article and applying them in homemade fashion, I taught my eldest daughter Anne to read when she was five years old. Well, you know Anne: she's ten now and reads anything and everything, all the time. Here is what

Bloomfield told the country's elementary English teachers twelve years ago: "The most serious drawback of all the English reading instruction known to me . . . is the drawback of the word-method. . . . The child who fails to grasp the content of what he reads is usually a poor reader in the mechanical sense. . . . If you want to play the piano with feeling and expression, you must master the keyboard and learn to use your fingers on it. The chief source of difficulty in getting the content of reading is imperfect mastery of the mechanics of reading. . . . We must train the child to respond vocally to the sight of letters. . . ."

And what did the teachers and reading experts do after the greatest scientist in the field had explained to them their mistake? Absolutely nothing. Except that several years later, in 1948, Dr. William S. Gray, of the University of Chicago, published a book, *On Their Own in Reading*. There, in the first chapter, was a lengthy quotation from Bloomfield's paper, followed by this statement: "The recent trend toward . . . the old alphabetic or phonic methods is viewed with alarm by educators. . . ."

The most conspicuous example of this deadly warfare between the entrenched "experts" and the advocates of common sense in reading is the reception of the primer *Reading With Phonics* by Hay and Wingo, published by the J. B. Lippincott Company. By some miracle, this textbook company decided to jump into the fray and publish the Hay-Wingo book, the only primer on the market today that is based firmly on the alphabetic-phonetic principle. Well, the book was duly reviewed in *Elementary English* magazine by Dr. Celia B. Stendler of the University of Illinois. I quote: "*Reading With Phonics* does not fit the modern conception of the place of phonics in a reading program. . . . One wonders at the naïveté of the authors. . . . One wonders, too, whether the authors have ever had the thrill of seeing a group of children learn to read by the use of modern methods. The zest with which these children approach reading and the zeal with which they read will almost certainly be lost if we turn the clock back twenty years with *Reading With Phonics.*" (This from someone who is all for turning the clock back 3,500 years!)

I'll have more to say later in this book about the Hay-Wingo primer which produces first-graders reading news items from the daily paper—and about the zest and zeal with which our children read:

Jack ran out to see the truck.
It was red and it was big—
very, very big.
It had come to take Jack
far away to his new home—
far away to his new home
on a big farm.

In doing research for this book, I ran into exactly the same kind of hostility. I wrote a letter to the National Council of Teachers of English, asking for information on the phonetic method of teaching reading. I got a brief reply, referring me to Dr. Paul Witty of Northwestern University (one of the top word-method people) and to a pamphlet "What About Phonics?" by Dr. Alvina Treut Burrows of New York University, which turned out to be violently anti-phonics. I also wrote the U.S. Office of Education. That time I got a somewhat longer reply, referring me to Dr. Edward W. Dolch of the University of Illinois (another well-known word-method man) and to the same biased pamphlet by Dr. Burrows.

At a later stage in my research I found an excellent paper by a Dr. Agnew who had compared the results of teaching reading in the schools of Durham and Raleigh, North Carolina. The monograph was published in 1939, at which time the schools in Durham produced splendid results by teaching phonics. So I wrote to the Superintendent of Schools in Durham, asking for information. The answer was that the teaching of phonics there had been discontinued seven years ago.

Then I ran across a book by the Italian educator Dr. Maria Montessori, published way back in 1912. Dr. Montessori, who was a world-famous progressive kindergarten teacher, taught her little Italian four-year-olds (!) the shapes and sounds of the letters of the alphabet and had them reading within weeks. I found that there was a Child Education Foundation in New York City carrying on Dr. Montessori's work. I wrote to them, asking about their method of teaching reading. The answer came back: "For a number of years we have found other methods to be more effective, so have not used Montessori."

Now that I have gone through dozens and dozens of books on reading, I know how well it all fits together. The primers and readers are keyed to the textbooks on how to teach reading, and the textbooks are all carefully written so that every teacher in the land is shielded from any information about how to teach children anything about letters and sounds.

It's a foolproof system all right. Every grade-school teacher in the country has to go to a teachers' college or school of education; every teachers' college gives at least one course on how to teach reading; every course on how to teach reading is based on a textbook; every one of those textbooks is written by one of the high priests of the word method. In the old days it was impossible to keep a good teacher from following her own common sense and practical knowledge; today the phonetic system of teaching reading is kept out of our schools as effectively as if we had a dictatorship with an all-powerful Ministry of Education.

And how do you convince thousands of intelligent young women that black is white and that reading has nothing to do with letters and sounds? Simple. Like this:

First, you announce loudly and with full conviction that our method of writing English is *not* based on pronunciation. Impossible, you say? Everybody knows that all alphabetic systems are phonetic? Oh no. I quote from page 297 of *Reading and the Educative Process* by Dr. Paul Witty of Northwestern University: "English is essentially an unphonetic language."

This is so ridiculous that it should be possible to just laugh about it and forget it. But the reading "experts" have created so much confusion that it's necessary to refute this nonsense. Well then: *All* alphabetic systems are phonetic; the two words mean the same thing. The only trouble is that English is a little more irregular than other languages. How much more has been established by three or four independent researchers. They all came up with the same figure. About 13 per cent of all English words are partly irregular in their spelling. The other 87 per cent follow fixed rules. Even the 13 per cent are not "unphonetic," as Dr. Witty calls it, but usually contain just one irregularly spelled vowel: *done* is pronounced "dun," *one* is pronounced "wun," *are* is pronounced "ar," and so on.

So our English system of writing is *of course* phonetic, but has a few more exceptions to the rules than other languages.

The next step in this great structure of nonsense and confusion is careful avoidance of the teaching of the letters:

"Current practice in the teaching of reading does not require a knowledge of the letters," says Dr. Donald D. Durrell of Boston University. "In remedial work, such knowledge is helpful."

"The skillful teacher will be reluctant to use any phonetic method with all children," says Dr. Witty.

"The child should be allowed to 'typewrite' only after he has a certain degree of ability in reading," says Dr. Guy L. Bond of the University of Minnesota. "Otherwise he is apt to become too conscious of the letter-by-letter elements of words."

And Dr. Roma Gans of Teachers College, Columbia University, tells us simply and starkly: "In recent years phonetic analysis of words at any level of the reading program fell into disrepute."

If they had their way, our teachers would *never* tell the children that there are letters and that each letter represents a sound. However, that isn't quite possible for the simple reason that a good many children are bright enough to find this out for themselves. So, if systematic phonetics or phonics from the outset is taboo, there has to be some sort of an answer when a child in second or third grade begins to notice that the first letter in *cat* is different from the first letter in *sat*. This is called "phonetic analysis" and—lo and behold!—it does get mentioned in the textbooks. For instance, if you turn to the index in *Learning to Read: a Handbook for Teachers* by Carter and McGinnis of the Psycho-Educational Clinic of the Western Michigan College of Education, you will find *one* lonely page reference to "phonetic analysis." Turning back to that page, you will learn that phonetic analysis "grows out of the fact that words are made up of letters or letter combinations that have known sounds. Phonetic analysis, then, is the process of associating the appropriate sounds with the printed forms. At this stage of development [third and fourth grade] emphasis should be placed upon beginning consonant sounds."

Otherwise, phonics is usually discussed in this literature as something that stupid and ignorant parents are apt to bring up. Yes, I am not joking: Our teachers are carefully coached in what to answer parents who complain about the abandonment of phonics.

For instance, let me quote from an "official" pamphlet on *Teaching Reading* by Dr. Arthur I. Gates (of Teachers College, Columbia University) published by the National Education Association. "When a mother storms to the school," writes Dr. Gates, "to protest delaying the starting of the child to read or what she imagines is the failure to teach good old phonics, it is likely that things have already happened in the home which are having a disadvantageous—indeed, sometimes a disastrous —influence on the pupil's efforts to learn. Had the mother understood the school's policy, provided it is a good one, the home life might have been organized in such a way as to assist the pupil greatly." In other words, if a parent complains that you don't teach her child the sounds of the letters, tell her the child can't read because she has made his home life unhappy.

That's what you get on the subject of phonetics in our literature on the teaching of reading. And what do the books contain instead? With what do they fill all those fat volumes with hundreds of pages if they don't mention the letters and sounds of the alphabet? Very simple: Those books are not about reading at all but about word guessing.

Because, you see, if a child isn't taught the sounds of the letters, then he has absolutely nothing to go by when he tries to read a word. All he can do is guess.

Suppose a child tries to read the sentence "I saw a kangaroo." Suppose he has never seen the word *kangaroo* before. If he has been trained in phonics, he simply "sounds out" the *k*, the *a*, the *ng*, the *a*, the *r*, and the *oo*, and reads "kangaroo" as easy as pie. ("Ah, kangaroo!" he says. Of course he has known the meaning of the word for years.) But if he has no training in phonics, if the meaning of the letters has been carefully hidden from him, he can only guess. How can he guess? Well, the educators say, he can guess from context. With the sentence "I saw a kangaroo" that is extremely difficult, however, because it could just as easily mean "I saw a giraffe" or "I saw a flea" or "I saw a piano." So, the next best thing, the child looks at the top of the page to see whether there is a picture. Usually in those factory-produced readers, when an animal is mentioned there is a picture of it somewhere on the page, so ten to one he'll find that the word means "kangaroo." And what if there isn't any picture? Well, then he has to rely on the sound of the first letter *k* if he knows *that*—or the length of the word—or its general shape—or just sheer luck. He might guess "kangaroo" or he might guess "plumber" or he might guess "forget-me-not" or—most likely—he might just sit there with a vacant look, waiting for the teacher to tell him what the word is. He knows very well she'll tell him eventually. Learning to read, he knows, is guessing or waiting until you are told what the word means.

You think I exaggerate? On the contrary: I am describing exactly what I saw in one classroom after another and what is detailed endlessly in all the textbooks on how to teach reading. Listen to them:

"Little is gained by teaching the child his sounds and letters as a first step to reading. More rapid results are generally obtained by the direct method of simply showing the word to the child and telling him what it is." (Irving H. Anderson and Walter F. Dearborn, *The Psychology of Teaching Reading.* Anderson is at the University of Michigan, Dearborn is a professor emeritus of Harvard.)

"The simplest solution when a child does not know a word is to *tell him what it says.*" (*Teaching Primary Reading* by Professor Edward A. Dolch, University of Illinois. The triumphant italics are by Dr. Dolch.)

"If the word is *daddy,* the pupil may give the word *father,* or *papa,* or *man,* since the basal meaning is the same. If the word is the noun *drink,* the pupil may say *water* or *milk* or some other fluid. Similarly, words related to a common situation or to a general topic, such as *cow, horse, pig, sheep, chicken,* are likely to be mistaken for each other.

"Errors of this type are frequently regarded as evidence of carelessness on the part of the pupil. In some instances he may be reprimanded for having made a 'wild guess,' when in fact, from the point of view of meaning the guess is not at all wild. In the early stages of learning to read frequent errors of this type are to be expected. They are . . . evidence of keen use of the device of guessing words from context." (Professor Arthur I. Gates, *The Improvement of Reading,* pp. 184-185. This is generally considered the most authoritative text of them all.)

And finally, here is a perfect summary of the situation from *Teaching the Child to Read* by Bond and Wagner. Professor Guy L. Bond is at the University of Minnesota.

The usual first unit of reading material is short and simple, rarely running more than four or five pages and introducing but few words. It is concerned with the common experiences of boys and girls of first-grade age whose activities are to be followed throughout the first year. Usually the boy and girl are introduced and some little story or incident told about them, mainly through the pictures with but little reading material. The pictures in the initial unit carry the story, and the words are so closely allied to the picture story that they usually can be guessed by the children. The teacher's major tasks during this time are to introduce the words in a meaningful fashion so that the children have contextual clues to aid them in "guessing" the word and to give repetition of the words so that those words may become the nucleus of a sight vocabulary. The words should be recognized as whole words. It is detrimental indeed to have the children spell or sound out the words at this stage.

Most of the modern readers have carefully worked out vocabulary controls so that the child will not encounter many new words in comparison to the number of words he actually reads. In various ways, which have been mentioned, the child is prepared for reading those words. In fact, he has been either given the name of the word or has been led to recognize the word before he meets it in his purposeful reading activity. When, however, he does have trouble with a word, that difficulty should not be focused upon as a difficulty. The teacher should at this stage tell him the word or lead him to guess it from the context.

What does all this add up to? It means simply and clearly that according to our accepted system of instruction, reading isn't taught at all. Books are put in front of the children and they are told to guess at the words or wait until Teacher tells them. But they are *not* taught to read—if by reading you mean what the dictionary says it means, namely, "get the meaning of writing or printing."

Now you will say that all this applies only to first grade. Not at all. If you think that after this preparatory guessing game reading begins in earnest in second grade, or in third, or in fourth, you are mistaken. Reading *never* starts. The guessing goes on and on and on, through grade school, through high school, through college, through life. It's all they'll ever know. They'll never really learn to read.

When I started to work with Johnny, I didn't quite realize all this. In my innocence, I gave him what I thought was an easy word for a twelve-year-old: *kid*. He stared at it for quite some time, then finally said "kind." I tell you, it staggered me. Nobody born and raised on the continent of Europe can easily grasp the fact that *anyone* can mistake *kid* for *kind*.

Later on, when I had done a good deal of phonics work with Johnny, I gave him, as an exercise, the word *razzing*. He hesitated, then read it as *realizing*. I said, "Don't guess, Johnny." I don't know how many hundreds of times I must have said to him, "Don't guess, Johnny." To my mind, a remedial reading case is someone who has formed the habit of guessing instead of reading.

You see, remedial reading cases are harder to teach than first-graders for the simple reason that they already have four or five or six years of guessing behind them. It usually takes at least a year to cure them of the habit. There wouldn't *be* any remedial reading cases if we started teaching reading instead of guessing in first grade. (Did I say this before? Forgive me. I have fallen into the habit of telling people the simple facts about reading over and over again. It seems to be the only way.)

And how do the educators explain all the thousands and thousands of remedial reading cases? This is what really got me mad. To them, failure in reading is *never* caused by poor teaching. Lord no, perish the thought. Reading failure is due to poor eyesight, or a nervous stomach, or poor posture, or heredity, or a broken home, or undernourishment, or a wicked stepmother, or an Oedipus complex, or sibling rivalry, or God knows what. The teacher or the school are never at fault. As to the textbook or the method taught to the teacher at her teachers' college—well, that idea has never yet entered the mind of anyone in the world of education.

In the book *How to Increase Reading Ability* by Professor Albert J. Harris of Queens College, New York City, there are long descriptions of remedial reading cases with all sorts of supposed causes and reasons—except the fact that Jimmie "confused *m* and *n*, *u* and *v*, *b* and *d*, *p* and *q*, *k* and *f*, and *y* and *w*," and Bruce "was unfamiliar with all of the short vowel sounds and with some consonant sounds." Fortunately Dr. Harris hit upon a phonics book, the Hegge-Kirk *Remedial Reading Drills,* and that was enough in most cases to bring those unhappy children up to par in their reading. (The Hegge-Kirk drills are what I finally used with Johnny. I'll come back to that book later on.)

There are also detailed case descriptions in *The Improvement of Reading* by Dr. Arthur I. Gates, the widely used text that I mentioned before. For instance, he tells about a ten-year-old girl who "often confused the sounds of *m* with *n* and had difficulty sounding the letter *y*. She also confused *l* with *i*." A seven-year-old boy, in a "test of ability to give sounds for individual letters, did not know the following: *f, d, z, r, m, l, q, u, w, h, n,* and *v*." An eight-year-old girl, "in a test where she was asked to give the sounds for individual letters, missed the following: *e, x, z, q,* and *g*."

And how does Dr. Gates account for all this? He obliges us by giving each of his cases a simple explanatory label. The first of these cases is labeled

Good Intellect, Poor Reading Techniques; Sibling Rivalry a Causal Factor.

The second case is headed

Reading Difficulties Resulting From Parental Interference.

The third is a case of

Poor Reading Resulting Largely From Parental Anxiety and Family Conflicts.

Dr. Gates, in contrast to Dr. Harris, didn't give his remedial cases phonics and consequently didn't help them; apparently he just gave the parents a good bawling out and let it go at that.

Most educators, however, don't go quite as far as that. They do use phonics in remedial cases—in dribs and drabs, testily, and rather furtively. Ordinary children, they say, shouldn't be deprived of the privilege of guessing words; but those poor unfortunate ones who didn't catch on to the guessing game—well, let's teach them the sounds of the letters as a last resort, purely as an emergency measure. (Remember the dictum by Dr. Durrell: "Current practice in the teaching of reading does not require a knowledge of the letters. In remedial work, such knowledge is helpful.") And so you find phonics discussed, if at all, tucked away in a section dealing with remedial reading with a careful explanation that this rather nasty medicine shouldn't be given to nice, average children who can guess the few hundred words contained in the "basal series."

The irony is that phonics is also recognized when it comes to the children *above* average—those that somehow learn to read properly and effectively *in spite of the way they were taught.* Those boys and girls, the reading experts tell us, have unusual phonic ability—which means that they managed to figure out by themselves which letter stands for which sound. Of course, you can't really read at all if you don't know that; but for our reading teachers it's a miraculous achievement, only to be explained by special gifts and extraordinary graces.

Not long ago, in January, 1954, Dr. Ruth Strang of Teachers College, Columbia University, published an article on the "Reading Development of Gifted Children" in *Elementary English.* "It may be," she wrote, "that the phonetic approach is more appropriate for the quick-learning than for the slow-learning child because of the former's greater analytical ability." (How she reconciled this observation with the fact that phonic methods are the only thing that works with retarded children I don't know.)

The article was based on statements by gifted boys and girls in junior high school. Here are some of them:

"How did I learn to read? First my grandmother taught me, then I caught on to certain words and got accustomed to sounding out words."

"By very small words and sentences. Also by syllables and the letter's sound."

"In first grade the teacher was dismissed for teaching phonetics, but I think phonetics has helped me very much in sounding out new words."

It seems clear to me that those bright twelve- and thirteen-year-olds know more about reading than all the faculties, students, and alumni of all of our teachers' colleges and schools of education taken together. And I *don't* think that those children are a bit more gifted than your Johnny. They were just luckier. Just lucky enough to find out in time that learning to read means learning to sound out words.

Chapter II

WHAT IS PHONICS?

Phonics isn't a word that is in common use. You probably think it's a technical subject that an ordinary person would find difficult to understand. Nonsense. Phonics is perfectly simple. Any normal adult can grasp it in one easy lesson.

Let's begin by distinguishing between phonics and phonetics. Phonetics, the dictionary says, is "the science dealing with speech sounds." It *is* a technical subject. Studying phonetics means studying a phonetic alphabet, diacritical marks, technical terms, and many other scientific tools and techniques. Phonetics is definitely *not* the thing to use if you want to teach small children to read and write. Therefore, about fifty years or so ago, those who believed in teaching reading by the phonetic method invented a way of doing it *without* using any special symbols or special terminology. They called this phonics; according to the dictionary, phonics is "simplified phonetics for teaching reading."

To understand phonics, forget all about our Chinese method of teaching reading and, in your imagination, start from scratch. Imagine, for instance, you are a Hottentot and want to learn how to read and write the Hottentot language. The natural method will be this: First, your teacher will make you aware of the individual sounds you make when you talk Hottentot. Second, he will show you the letter symbols that represent each of those sounds. Third, he will teach you how to write these symbols and combine them into words—and, *at the same time,* how to read them.

In a language with a perfectly phonetic alphabet, this is a very short and simple process. Dr. Frank C. Laubach, famous for his work in teaching half the world to read and write, always starts by working out a phonetic alphabet for the language he is dealing with, and then teaches the natives in very short order how to read and write it. For instance, in his book *Teaching the World to Read,* he writes of the application of the method to the most widely spoken dialect of the Philippines. "It is easy," he writes, "for a man with average intelligence to learn to read in one day by using these lessons. Many people have learned to read all of the letters in two hours, some even in one hour."

Yes, if you have a language with a perfectly phonetic alphabet, you are in a sort of dream world, where teaching to read and write is no problem at all. This is true, for instance, in a few European languages that are blessed with an almost perfect system, namely, Spanish, Finnish, and Czech. (Many years ago, when I was about fifteen, I took a semester's course in Czech; I have since forgotten everything about the language itself, but I still remember how the letters are pronounced, plus the simple rule that all words have the accent on the first syllable. Armed with this knowledge, I once surprised a native of Prague by reading aloud from a Czech newspaper. "Oh, you know Czech?" he asked. "No, I don't understand a word of it," I answered. "I can only read it.")

But let's get back from this dream world to the harsh reality of English. Let's begin with the sounds you make when you talk.

How many of those sounds are there? Scientists don't fully agree on that point; besides, not everybody speaking English makes the same sounds. However, if you want to arrive at a *practical* number, there is a simple way: Count the items in the pronunciation key of an ordinary desk-size dictionary or handbook of English and see how many different sounds have a special symbol assigned to them. For example, the pronunciation key in the *Thorndike-Barnhart High School Dictionary* has 43 items; the pronunciation key in Perrin's *Writer's Guide and*

Index to English also has 43. However, each of these books includes one item the other one does not: Perrin lists *hw* for the first sound in *wheel* and *whether,* which isn't given in Thorndike-Barnhart; and Thorndike-Barnhart has the *a* sound in *care* and *air,* which isn't in Perrin. (Perrin adds at the end of his list: "An *r* following a vowel changes the vowel's sound, as in *care, sere, core, sure,* but a separate symbol is not used to represent the change.")

From these two typical sources you therefore get forty-four sounds that can be distinguished in English—or rather, forty-four symbols that you would need if you wanted to construct an English phonetic alphabet.

Actually, as you know, we have not forty-four letters but twenty-six. Not only that, three of our twenty-six letters are superfluous, namely, *c, q,* and *x.* (*C* has the sound of either *k* or *s, qu* stands for *kw,* and *x* sounds like *ks* in *six* and like *gz* in *exist.*) This leaves us with twenty-three letters to represent forty-four sounds. And there you have the basic reason for our whole reading problem.

Nevertheless, ridiculous as this setup is, it's the system we've got, so let's see how it can be taught. Let's begin, like the Hottentot, the Filipino, or the lucky Finnish, Czech, or Spanish-speaking child, by learning the letters or letter combinations that stand for each of our forty-four sounds. Here they are:

Twenty-five of the forty-four sounds are consonants. Eighteen of these come in pairs, "soft" and "hard":

B and *p* as in *bib* and *pup.*
D and *t* as in *dad* and *toot.*
G and *k* as in *gag* and *kick.*
V and *f* as in *valve* and *fluff.*
Z and *s* as in *zig-zag* and *Sis.*
Th ("soft") and *th* ("hard") as in *thither* and *thistle.*
W and *wh* as in *wayward* and *whistle.*
J and *ch* as in *jam* and *choo-choo-train.*
Zh and *sh* as in *treasure* and *trash.* (The "zh" is the biggest

absurdity in our crazy system: there is no proper way of spelling this sound at all. It's the sound in *Asia, television, hosiery,* and many other common words like *measure, pleasure, usual, casual,* and *leisure.* Noah Webster in 1783 thought up the symbol *zh* for it, and almost every textbook writer and dictionary maker has been using it since.)

Then there are six consonants often called semivowels: *l* as in *lull, m* as in *ma'm, n* as in *nun, r* as in *rare, y* as in *yo-yo,* and *ng,* which is *not* a combination of *n* and *g* but an altogether different sound. (Listen to yourself when you say *singing* or *banging.*) The sound of *ng* also occurs before the sound of *k* in words spelled with *nk—drink, mink, pink.*

Eighteen plus six makes twenty-four consonants. The twenty-fifth consonant is *h*—as in *his* or *hers.*

Now let's look at the remaining nineteen vowel sounds and the symbols that represent them in writing. Before we do that, however, let's do a simple bit of arithmetic. So far we have used up nineteen letters to write our twenty-five consonants, namely, *b, c, d, f, g, h, j, k, l, m, n, p, r, s, t, v, w, y,* and *z.* In addition. there are two more superfluous letters that also represent consonant combinations: *q* and *x.* In other words, we have used up twenty-one of the twenty-six letters to write the consonants, which leaves us with exactly five—*a, e, i, o, u*—to deal with nineteen vowel sounds. And this is where English spelling gets really nasty.

Here are the nineteen vowel sounds:

First, there are the five so-called short vowels, as in *bag, beg, big, bog, bug.*

Second, there are the five so-called long vowels as in *mate, mete, mite, mote, mute.* As you see, these long vowels are spelled like the short ones, but with a silent *e* after the consonant following the vowel. They can also be spelled in a variety of other ways: You can use *ai* and *ay* for the long *a; ee* and *ea* for the long *e; ie, y,* and *ye* for the long *i; oa, oe,* and *ow* for the long *o;* and *ue* and *ew* for the long *u.*

Next, we have three diphthongs (combinations of two sounds) each with two different spellings: *au* as in *Paul* and *crawl, ou* as in *spouse* and *cow,* and *oi* as in *noise* and *boy.*

Next, a long and a short *oo,* as in *Rube* and *boob,* and *whoosh* and *push.*

Next, the sound of *ah* as in *pa* and *ma, bar* and *car.*

Next, two *r* vowels: *air* as in *Fair heirs dare swear,* and *er* as in *Girls prefer fur.*

Finally, the all-purpose muttering vowel we use in unaccented syllables regardless of the spelling—the *a* in *drama,* the *e* in *item,* the *i* in *devil,* the *o* in *button,* the *u* in *circus.*

And that's the end of our forty-four-item list—a highly imperfect system, to be sure, but nevertheless a system that can be explained and taught without throwing up your hands in despair and going back to Chinese word learning.

What's the best way of teaching this system? To find out, I compared the most important methods used during the past 170 years—Noah Webster's *Blue-Backed Speller,* the McGuffey Readers, the once-famous Beacon Readers, today's Hay-Wingo method, Bloomfield method, Hegge-Kirk method, and others. I discovered a great family resemblance among all those methods and a common sequence underlying them all. This is not surprising since it's a natural sequence based on our imperfect system of spelling.

As I showed you, there are two main things wrong with our alphabet and our system of spelling. One is that we have only about half as many letters as we have sounds—which means that half the symbols a child has to learn consist not of one letter but two—like *ay, ea, sh, ch,* and so on. The other trouble is that some of our most important single letters are used to spell two or more entirely different sounds, namely, the five vowels *a, e, i, o, u,* and the consonants *c* and *g.*

Therefore, if you want to teach a child to read without utterly confusing him, you have to start him with single letters that stand for single sounds, then go on to sounds spelled by two-letter or three-letter combinations, and finally teach him that some of the letters do not spell one sound but two.

The catch in this, however, is that you can't teach a child to read without letting him read words. And every word in English contains a vowel. So you *have* to start with teaching the child the letters *a, e, i, o, u* in spite of the fact that each of them spells a long *and* a short vowel. The only way to solve this problem is to begin by teaching the child only the five *short* vowels (which are far more common than the long ones) and postpone the long vowels until a much later stage.

All of which means that the natural sequence of *any* phonic method is this:

Step One: The five short vowels and all consonants spelled by single letters.

Step Two: Consonants and consonant combinations spelled with two or three letters.

Step Three: Vowels and vowel combinations spelled with two or three letters.

Step Four: The five long vowels.

Step Five: Irregular spellings.

These five steps, as I said, occur in all phonic systems of teaching a child to read English. (There are some so-called phonic readers on the market that do not follow this pattern, but they can hardly be called phonic by any proper definition of the word.)

Naturally I don't expect you to be satisfied with this brief description. You are entitled to a reasonably complete recipe for teaching a child to read—a section of this book that you can put to immediate practical use. So here is a simple system that will do the job. I don't offer this system as "the Flesch method" or anything like that; as I explained, it is simply the common core of all major phonic systems ever offered to the public.

To teach Johnny to read, do this:

Begin by teaching him the letters *a, e, i, o, u* and their short vowel sounds. The classic way of doing that is to show him each letter with a picture of a familiar object whose name begins with the short vowel. For example, the Hay-Wingo book starts with pictures of an apple, an elephant, an Indian, an ostrich, and an umbrella. (As you realize, the names of the letters A, E, I, O, U are not the short vowel sounds but the long vowel sounds. Since this is apt to confuse Johnny, you'd perhaps better not teach him the alphabet until a little later.)

With the five short vowels, teach Johnny the following seventeen consonants: *b, d, f, g, h, j, l, m, n, p, r, s, t, v, w, y, z*. Again, you might use pictures like a bell for *b*, a doll for *d*, a fish for *f* and so on. Teach Johnny only the "hard" sound of *g* as in *girl* and don't confuse him with words like *gem* or *gingerbread*. (He'll learn those much later.) Similarly, teach him only the *s* that sounds like *ss* and not the *s* that sounds like *z*. Teach him only the consonant *y* as in *yes, yet,* and *yesterday,* and not the vowel *y* that sounds like *i*.

To fix these twenty-two sounds and letters in Johnny's memory, let him read *and write from dictation* as many one-syllable words as possible that contain these sounds. (Use words that begin with the vowels or with any of the consonants and end with *b, d, g, ll, m, n, p, ss,* or *t*.) This first stage is tremendously important because Johnny must learn, once and for all, that words are written by putting down letters from left to right, and that they are read in the same direction.

After Johnny has gone through *pup, Sam, him, Bill, pad, run, bib, tub, web, Ted,* and so forth, and has reached the point of reading these words without trouble, give him one more simple consonant sound—the sound of *k*. Explain to him that before *a, o,* and *u* this sound is spelled *c*, but before *e* and *i* it is spelled *k*. *After* a short vowel it is usually spelled *ck*.

Now Johnny has reached the second step: combinations of consonant sounds. Those at the end of a word will be easier for him than those at the beginning of a word. So start him with two-letter consonant combinations at the end of a word: *ft* as in *lift*, *lk* as in *milk*, *lm* as in *elm*, *lp* as in *help*, *lt* as in *belt*, *mp* as in *lamp*, *nd* as in *hand*, *nt* as in *tent*, *pt* as in *kept*, *sk* as in *desk*, *sp* as in *lisp*, *st* as in *nest*.

At this point, explain to Johnny the rule about the letter *s* at the end of a word: After the consonants *f*, *k*, *p*, and *t*, it stands for the hissing *ss* sound, but after all other sounds it stands for the *z* sound.

Next, teach him the following consonant combinations at the end of words: *ng* as in *ring*, *nk* as in *pink*, *x* as in *fox*, *sh* as in *fish*.

Next, take up consonant combinations at the beginning of words. Here is your list: *bl* as in *blink*, *br* as in *brag*, *cl* as in *clash*, *cr* as in *crack*, *dr* as in *drink*, *fl* as in *flag*, *fr* as in *frog*, *gl* as in *glad*, *gr* as in *grab*, *pl* as in *plug*, *pr* as in *press*, *sc* as in *scamp*, *sk* as in *skip*, *sl* as in *sled*, *sm* as in *smack*, *sn* as in *snap*, *sp* as in *spill*, *st* as in *stamp*, *sw* as in *swim*, *tr* as in *trip*, *tw* as in *twin*. Then there is *scr* as in *scrap*, *shr* as in *shrimp*, *spl* as in *splash*, *spr* as in *spring*, and *str* as in *stretch*. To teach Johnny these sound combinations, give him words that become other words when a second consonant is put in front: *lap* and *slap*, *ring* and *bring*, *rug* and *drug*, *nip* and *snip*. Johnny will like reading aloud words like *snack*, *crack*, and *plop*.

Next, take some other consonant sounds and combinations at the beginning of words: *qu* as in *quack*, *wh* as in *whiff*, "soft" *th* as in *that* and "hard" *th* as in *thick*. Then take the sound of *ch* and explain to Johnny that it is usually spelled *ch* at the beginning of a word and *tch* at the end.

Now Johnny is through with the second step. He can read or write from dictation all regularly spelled words that contain any consonant and any of the five short vowels. There are also a number of two-syllable words you can give him at this point: *basket*, *redskin*, *frosting*, *lemon*, *napkin*, *rabbit*, *chicken*, *locket*, *wicked*, *robin*, and so on.

Next, Step Three: Teach Johnny vowels and vowel combinations spelled with two letters.

First, the *ee* sound, spelled *ee* as in *sheep* or *ea* as in *meal*. This is your chance to tell Johnny about words that sound alike but are spelled differently to distinguish between different meanings, like *meet* and *meat, feet* and *feat, see* and *sea, flee* and *flea*. (He'll like learning these pairs and make a game out of it.) Tell him also about the words rhyming with *ee* but spelled with only one *e—be, he, me, she, we*.

Next, teach Johnny the *oo* sound—short as in *book* and *look,* or long as in *moon* and *spoon*.

The *ah* sound as in *car, park, lark,* and *pa, ma*.

The *or* sound as in *lord, fort, born*.

The *er* sound as in *bird, hurt, her*.

The *oi* sound as in *oil* and *boil, toy* and *boy*. Explain to Johnny that it's usually *oi* inside a word and *oy* at the end.

The *ou* sound as in *house* and *cow*. Again, explain to him that it's usually *ou* inside a word and *ow* at the end.

The *au* sound, usually spelled *au* in the middle as in *Paul* and *aw* at the end as in *raw*. This is the point to teach Johnny the spellings *all, alt, alk* as in *hall, salt, talk*.

The *ai* sound, usually spelled *ai* inside a word and *ay* at the end. Teach Johnny also the slightly different sound in *air, pair, fair*.

The long *i* sound spelled *ie* or *y* as in *pie, dry, my, shy*. Take this opportunity to teach Johnny words like *mind, kind, bind,* and *mild, wild*.

The long *o* sound, spelled *oa* as in *boat, oe* as in *toe, ow* as in *blow,* or simply *o* as in *go, so,* and *no*. Tell Johnny about such words as *old, hold, sold,* and *bolt, colt*.

Finally, the long *u* sound, spelled *ew* as in *new* or *ue* as in *true blue*. Don't forget pairs like *flew* and *flue, dew* and *due*.

By now, Johnny has a tremendous reading and writing vocabulary. He can also figure out a long list of two-syllable and three-syllable words like *oatmeal, mailbox, swallow, sheepish,* murmuring, sunbeam, untrue, leapfrog, murderer, bamboo, cartoon, grandfather, hamburger, restlessness, flamingo, kangaroo, curlicue, and *Easter bonnet.*

Now comes Step Four: The long vowel sounds, spelled *a, e, i, o, u.* The easiest way to teach Johnny these is to show him the effect of a silent *e* added to a word. In other words, teach him to read and write *fad—fade, pet—Pete, pin—pine, rob—robe, cut—cute.* (If he has learned the alphabet by now, tell him that the silent *e* "makes the letter say its name.")

After Johnny has learned the silent *e,* show him that the syllable *ing* will also make the vowel sound long: *rate—rating, file—filing* and so on. Explain to him the important rule that if you want to keep the vowel short in such *ing* words, you have to double the final consonant before adding the *ing.* For example: *bedding, shipping, trapping, humming, brimming, trimming.*

Next, teach Johnny final *y* as in *lady, rainy, handy.* Show him that the double-consonant rule applies here too, as in *nutty, sunny,* and *foggy.* Explain to him that the plural of *lady* is spelled *ladies,* of *body, bodies,* and so on. Tell him about *lazy, lazier, laziest,* and *lazily.*

Next, take up ending *ed,* again with the double-consonant rule, as in *matted, rugged, robbed.*

Then, final *er* and *le,* again with the double-consonant rule, as in *rubber, trigger, settle, middle.*

Finally, teach Johnny *ce* as in *rice, ge* as in *age, se* as in *cheese,* and *the* as in *loathe.* Give him word pairs like *pack* and *pace, hug* and *huge, bath* and *bathe.* Give him also some examples of *dge* as in *badge* and *hedge.*

Now you are through with the fourth step. Johnny has learned to read and write practically all the words that follow *some* spelling rule. The fifth step will be easy for him. He'll learn words in *sion* and *tion,* words in *ight, ought* and *caught,* silent *k* in *knife,* silent *w* in *write,* silent *t* in *whistle,* silent *l* in *calf,* silent *g* in *gnu,* words like *head* and *bread, word* and *worm, chief* and *thief, break* and *steak,* and so on.

And that's all. Everything else will come to Johnny automatically, because he can now read anything.

It took me five pages to set down the phonic method of teaching Johnny to read. Complicated, you say? I don't think so. I have seen six-year-olds getting the hang of it in a few months.

Anyway, it's not a question of speed. The point is that this method is *guaranteed.* A child who has been taught this way can read. Millions of children taught the other way can't.

Chapter III

WHY JOHNNY CAN'T SPELL

You were probably surprised to see so much about spelling in the last chapter. All the spelling rules that I told you to teach Johnny, and my emphasis on letting him not only read the practice words but also write them from dictation—why, you may have thought that I am mixing up two things that have nothing to do with each other. Reading is one thing, you thought, spelling is another. It's enough of a problem to bring Johnny up to par with his reading, so why try to make a crack speller out of him at the same time?

Yes, that's the common attitude. Reading and spelling are considered two different "subjects." To learn reading, you do this; to learn spelling, you do that.

It is one of the main points of this book that that attitude is all wrong. Reading and spelling are two sides of the same thing, and the trouble starts as soon as you separate the two. The only way to teach reading is by teaching spelling *at the same time.*

The primitive people taught all over the world by Dr. Laubach were not really "taught to read": they were taught to "read-and-write." With a phonetic alphabet and the phonic method it's simply a question of overcoming illiteracy and learning which letter stands for which sound. Once you know that, you can read *and* spell.

I am sure the same thing is true in such languages as Spanish, Finnish, and Czech. I *know* that this is so because it's even true in German, which has a far from perfect alphabet and quite

33

a few irregular spellings. Even so, spelling difficulties are as rare in Germany and Austria as serious reading problems. To be sure, lots of people in those countries occasionally misspell some of the more outlandish words; but the ordinary person is hardly ever bothered by spelling difficulties in ordinary German words. A German typist has a little book on spelling, syllabication, and punctuation in her desk drawer, but if she is any good at all, she hardly ever refers to it.

As to German children, they do sometimes ask their parents how to spell a certain word. The usual answer is "Why, it's spelled just as it sounds" and that takes care of the matter. In our country, a mother who has been taught by the phonic method and is asked "How do you spell *Amazon?*" may also answer "Just as it sounds, dear." But she'll hardly give that answer more than once. The blank look she gets in return will make her realize that such an answer means absolutely nothing to a child who has never heard of the phonic principle. The average child is like the G.I. "non-reader" whose telling remark is quoted in an article on remedial reading in the January 1952 *Independent School Bulletin:* "Until I had the sounds for the letters I had never known that the letters in a word had anything to do with pronouncing it."

Of course, it is true that we don't have a perfect phonetic alphabet and that even the phonic method will only get you that far in spelling. But how far is "that far"? If you look into the history of English spelling, you will learn that "that far" is very far indeed. Up until about 1600 a knowledge of the letters and the sounds plus a few basic spelling rules would take anybody all the way. Equipped with this basic knowledge he was sure to be free from spelling problems for the rest of his life.

How come? The answer is simple, but rather startling to a modern person to whom correct spelling is something as fully accepted as not eating peas off your knife or being quiet in church. Up to about 1600 the idea of correct spelling was unknown. Literate English-speaking people were perfectly free to spell the words they wrote any which way, as the spirit moved them. Spelling was a means to an end, a device to make words understandable to a reader. Nobody cared about correctness—in fact, as I said, the concept of correctness was totally unknown. Shakespeare spelled freely; so did Milton, who had a way of writing *mee* instead of *me* and *shee* instead of *she* whenever he felt the pronoun needed special emphasis.

To make this quite clear to you, I dug up some good examples of sixteenth-century English spelling. The first is from the diary of Henry Machyn, quoted in Henry C. Wyld's *History of Modern Colloquial English*. "Machyn's work," says Wyld, "is a priceless monument of the English of the Middle Class Londoner, with no particular education or refinement." This is what Machyn wrote in his diary in 1557:

The xvj day of June my yong duke of Norfoke rod abrod and at Stamford-hylle my lord havying a dage hangyng on ys Sadylle bow, and by mysse-fortune dyd shutte yt, and yt on of ys men that ryd afor, and so by myssforten ys horse dyd flyng as so he hangyd on by on of ys sterope, and so thatt the horse knokyd ys brayns owt with flyngyng out with ys leges.

Last day of June. The sam day the kyng grace rod on untyng into the forest and kyllyd a grett stage with gones.

The iiij of August was the masse of requiem for my lade prenses of Cleyff . . . and ther my lord abbott of Westmynster mad a godly sermon as ever was mad, and the byshope of London song masse in ys myter, [and after] masse my lord byshope and my lord abbott mytered dyd cense the corsse, and afterward she was caried to her tomb [where] she leys with a herse-cloth of gold the wych lyys [over her]; and ther all her hed offerers brake their stayffes, her hussears brake ther rodes, and all they cast them into her tombe; the wyche was covered her corsse with blake, and all the lordes and knyghts and gentyllmen and gentill-vomen dyd offer, and after amasse a grett dener at my lord abbots, and my lade of Wynchester was the cheyff [mourner] and my lord admeroll and lord Dacre wher of ether syde of my lade of Wynchester and so they whent in order to dinner.

You see what I mean about freedom in spelling? Machyn spells it twice *abbott* with two *t*'s and the third time he writes *abbots* with one *t;* he writes *mysse-fortune,* and a few words later in the same sentence he spells is *myssforten;* he writes *dener* and at the end of the same sentence he makes it *dinner.* And of course, since he drops his aitches in speaking, cockney-fashion, he writes *ys* for *his,* and *untyng* for *hunting;* then he *adds* an *h* where it doesn't belong and writes *hussears* for *ushers.* Having never heard of "correct" spelling, he spells *stirrup* "sterope," *princess* "prenses," and *admiral* "admeroll."

Machyn, however, was not an educated man. The argument wouldn't be complete if I couldn't prove to you that educated sixteenth-century Englishmen too spelled any which way, whatever letter combinations happened to suit their fancy. So here are the first few paragraphs of the last will and testament of Sir Thomas Gresham, the great banker and financial adviser to Queen Elizabeth. His will is dated July 4, 1575:

In the name of God, Amen. The fourth day of July in the seaventene yere of oure Souvereyen lady Elyssabethe, by the grace of God quene of Ingland, France, and Ireland, deffeander of the faith, &c., and in the yere of our lorde God 1575, I Sir Thomas Gresham, knighte, calling to minde howe certteyne it is that all mankinde shall leve and departe ought of this transsitorye lieffe, and how uncerteyne the tyme and mannor thereof is, and for dispossinge of siche goodes as it haithe pleassed Almighttie God to make me posseas in this worlde in soche wysse as the same maye be to Godes glorye and to the quyeat of soche as after my death shalbe intiteled to have the same with ought contencion, doe therefore macke and declare my teastament and last will in manner and form folloinge. First, I bequeath my sowle to Almyghttie God my Creator and Redeemer, trusting by the meritts onely of Cristes passion and death to be saved. My boddy I doe bequeathe to the yerthe, to be burryead in St. Tellyns in the parrishe that I doo now dwele in, in soche wysse as seame good by the discreassione of my welbeloved wyffe my sole executrixe. And I geve and bequeathe to my welbeloved wiffe the lady Ann Gresham, towardes the payments of my deates and for the perfformans of this my last will, all my hoole goodes, as reddy monny, playte, jeuellis, chaynes of golde, with all my stocke of shepe and other cattayle that I have wythe in the realme of Inglonde. Item, I geve and bequeathe to my preantysse William Gilbert fourtie poundes. To my prentysse Phillipe Celye fourtie poundes. To my preantysse John Smythe fourtie poundes. To my preantisse Phillipe Gilmor fortye poundes. . . .

You would expect, wouldn't you, the last will of one of the leading men of Elizabethan England to be a model of correct spelling. But, as I said, Sir Thomas Gresham was as unfamiliar with the idea of correctness in spelling as everyone else in his day. So he writes *preantysse* in one sentence, *prentysse* in the next, and *preantisse* in the third. He writes *certteyne* and *uncerteyne* in the same sentence; he spells *mannor* and *manner, wythe* and *with, wyffe* and *wiffe, fourtie* and *fortie, I doe* and *I doo*. And without the slightest self-consciousness he spells *yere, quyeat, perfformans,* and *shepe*.

Why am I giving you these quaint old examples? Because to understand the problem of spelling you have to realize what it was like when English spelling was absolutely free. There simply was no set way to spell *princess* or *abbot* or *sheep,* but everybody who was literate at all was expected to know his letter sounds and to spell solely by ear. Consequently he was also expected and accustomed to "read by ear," that is, to pronounce the words aloud or at least to sound them out in his mind.

There were two stages in the transition between the happy spelling freedom of sixteenth-century England and our fixed word-picture reading and spelling of today. The first was the limitation of writers to one spelling only for each word. No more choice between *fourtie* and *fortye* and *fourtye* and *fortie*: the spelling is now *forty* and everything else is wrong.

The one man mostly responsible for this change was Dr. Samuel Johnson, the dictionary maker. Somehow or other people took to Johnson's spellings, and the notion sprung up

that all other spellings should be abandoned. Not that Johnson was particularly consistent, though: he spelled it *moveable*
but *immovable, downhill* but *uphill, distil* but *instill, install*
but *reinstal, sliness* but *slyly, deign* but *disdain,* and *conceit*
and *deceit* but *receipt.* As you can see, quite a few of his incon-
sistencies are still with us today.

After Johnson came Noah Webster, who was quite fanatical
about *his* "correct spellings" and made Americans even more
"correct-spelling-conscious" than Englishmen.

And so here we are today, with free and easy spelling long
forgotten and everybody fully obedient to the spellings given
in the dictionary.

However, if we still had the phonic method of teaching
reading—together with teaching spelling, of course—it would
still be possible to become an almost perfect speller without
too much effort. We would just have to learn which letter
stands for which sound, plus a few basic spelling rules, plus the
one among several possible spellings that is given in the dictionary. That's a tougher job than the one Henry Machyn
and Sir Thomas Gresham were faced with, but it's not insuper-
able. Anyone with a firm phonic foundation can pick up the
accepted spellings in his reading, without laboriously fixing
each individual word picture in his mind.

But we *don't* teach reading by way of phonics any more. So
how do today's American children learn to spell? Even after I
found out about the whole-word method of teaching reading
and was about halfway through the research for this book, I still
in my ex-European innocence believed that when it comes to
spelling, our children finally get *some* phonics. I simply
couldn't imagine that anyone can learn to spell at all without
learning the pronunciation of the letters.

Well, I learned different. We have reached the point where
phonics has been driven out even of the teaching of spelling.
Then how can you teach a child that *princess* is spelled *p, r,
i, n, c, e, s, s?* Like this (I am quoting from the latest edition

of the official manual for elementary-school teachers, published
by the Education Department of the State of New York):

> Following are proposals for conducting a spelling program.
>
> 1. Lead the children to feel that spelling is important. . . .
> 2. Combine spelling with vocabulary and dictionary work . . .
> arousing the children's interest in individual words and in lan-
> guage in general. . . .
> 3. When teaching the correct spelling of a word to children, do
> five things:
>> a. Pronounce and enunciate the word clearly yourself while
>> the children watch your lips.
>> b. Use the word in a sentence . . . to be sure that the children
>> will understand one meaning of the word.
>> c. Pronounce the word a second time, writing it on the black-
>> board as you say it so the children can see it. Have them pro-
>> nounce the word.
>> d. Be sure the children can pronounce the word correctly. . . .
>> e. Urge the children to notice carefully the way the word
>> *looks* before they try to reproduce it on paper.
> 4. Use the word in context both before and after the correct
> spelling is presented. This deepens understanding on the part of
> the children as to what the word means.
> 5. Emphasize the syllabication of words. . . .
> 6. Provide at frequent intervals for each child to review his own
> list of words that are hard for him.

As you can see from this, the currently accepted teaching of
spelling (and surely New York State is typical of the nation in
this matter) consists in teaching first the meaning of the word—
which hasn't a thing to do with the spelling—and secondly, its
pronunciation. Now the pronunciation, of course, *is* a help in
spelling, but only if you know how to transcribe the sounds
into letters. This the children in the State of New York—
and in the other forty-seven states—are *not* taught; in fact,
teachers are warned against giving them any phonics in connection with spelling. Says the State of New York manual (and

I still quote): "Phonetic analysis is not a very effective way to teach the spelling of words. English is a notoriously non-phonetic language."

Which brings us right back to where we started in the first chapter. And what's the result of this modern method of teaching spelling? Look into any college handbook of English and you'll find a long list of common spelling errors college students are apt to make. Here are some current campus favorites:

accerate (for *accurate*)
Britian (for *Britain*)
buisness (for *business*)
calvary (for *cavalry*)
considable (for *considerable*)
definate (for *definite*)
differnt (for *different*)
dispite (for *despite*)
docter (for *doctor*)
Febuary (for *February*)
fourty (for *forty*)
grammer (for *grammar*)
irrevelant (for *irrelevant*)
libary (for *library*)
medecine (for *medicine*)

miricle (for *miracle*)
ocassion (for *occasion*)
preperation (for *preparation*)
privalege (for *privilege*)
proffessor (for *professor*)
reconize (for *recognize*)
seperate (for *separate*)
similiar (for *similar*)
suceed (for *succeed*)
suprise (for *surprise*)
tendancy (for *tendency*)
tradegy (for *tragedy*)
villiage (for *village*)
visable (for *visible*)
writting (for *writing*)

I give you this list of familiar mistakes because it shows quite clearly what's the trouble with our teaching of spelling. The trouble is *not* that people can't spell the famous bugaboos and spelling-bee words like *caoutchouc, eleemosynary, pterodactyl,* or *tintinnabulation.* The trouble is that with our system of teaching even the simplest words present difficulties that shouldn't ever arise. A person who was taught phonics in first grade wouldn't misspell *any* of the words on my list. Let me show you why this is so. Let's look at a few of these words a little more closely.

There are, for instance, the common misspellings "writting," "ocassion," and "suceed." The reason for "writting" is of course that *written* has two *t*'s and so the poor speller has a dim notion that there are also two *t*'s *in writing. Occasion,* he knows, has two *c*'s or two *s*'s. But which? He guesses, and nine times out of ten he guesses wrong. As to *succeed,* he has a feeling that there *can't* be a double *c* in English; isn't it always *ck?* So he writes "suceed."

A person trained in phonics can't possibly make any of these mistakes. He *knows.* He knows that a double consonant results in a short vowel sound and that therefore "writting" would rhyme with *sitting;* he knows that the *zh* sound in *occasion* can only be spelled with a single *s* and that "ocassion" would rhyme with *fashion;* he knows that the sound of *ks* as in *success* is sometimes spelled *cc* as in *accent, flaccid,* and *accident.*

Next, let's take misspellings like "Britian," "tradegy," and "similiar." Here again, the person who knows phonics can't go wrong. He knows that "Britian" would rhyme with *mission,* "tradegy" with *strategy,* and "similiar" with *familiar.* Why do people make mistakes like that? The only explanation, again, is our method of teaching spelling. Remember Point 3e. of that benighted spelling program of New York State: "Urge the children to notice carefully the way the word looks." Our children, in other words, are deliberately trained to spell by the eye rather than by the ear. The result is that they become so familiar with certain common endings that they think they see them even in words where they don't fit the pronunciation. The ending *ian* is far more common than *ain;* the ending *gy* occurs in *elegy, prodigy, energy,* and *effigy;* the ending *liar* seems more "probable" than *lar* because it occurs in *peculiar* and *familiar.* I deliberately said "seems more probable" in the last sentence. Our spelling, just as our reading, is wholly based on word guessing. For a guess, "Britian" isn't at all bad; the only trouble is that it's wrong.

And now let's look at some other words on our list. "Febuary," "reconize," "considable"—all the books will tell you that the reason for these misspellings is poor pronunciation. Teach the children to say "Febrrew-ary," "recogg-nize," and "consid-urrable," they tell you, and that will take care of the mis-spellings. Unfortunately it isn't so and people go through their whole lives spelling it "libary" although they have been told a thousand times that it is "librrrary." Why do they? And—what's even more remarkable—why do they write "definate," "grammer," and "miricle," although their eyes have looked at *definite, grammar,* and *miracle* millions of times?

They do because their whole-word training makes a tre-mendous difference in their mental habits. Anyone who has started with phonics in first grade goes through life reading every single word he reads letter by letter. He does this fan-tastically fast, and quite unconsciously, but nevertheless he does it. Every time he reads *miracle,* he *sees* the *a;* every time he reads *definite,* he *sees* the second *i.* No wonder he knows how to spell these words; he simply can't read without taking in every single letter. He has done this since he was six years old and has never in his life read a single word by just taking in its general shape and guessing what it might mean.

But our schools, as I said before, train our children in just that—word guessing. The whole literature on the teaching of reading deals basically with the problem of how to make a child read *miracle* without seeing the *a,* and *definite* without seeing the second *i.* It's possible to do that—the majority of today's Americans have never done anything else—but the results are disastrous. They can't read; they can't spell. Not only that, they can't even *learn* how to spell properly because they have been equipped with mental habits that are almost impos-sible to break—except by starting all over again from scratch and relearning to read and write English with phonics.

Chapter IV

A COW AND CONSEQUENCES

How did this whole thing come about? Here I have spent a good many pages telling you that there is only one way to teach reading and that all our schools obstinately persist in using another method that doesn't work. On the face of it, that's an incredible accusation. Surely, you say, modern education is based on science: there must have been experiments and tests and laboratory studies and years of weighing the advantages of the new method and the disadvantages of the old one. This vastly important shift cannot just have sprung full-grown from the brain of some educator; it must be the result of modern educational psychology.

Which is exactly what you will find in the books and articles of the educators. Here, for instance, is a brand-new book, *Educational Psychology* by Dr. Lee J. Cronbach of the University of Illinois, published in 1954. The teaching of reading is discussed right in the first chapter, "How Psychology Contributes to Education." This is the story, according to Dr. Cronbach:

It once seemed completely obvious . . . that you have to read words before you can read sentences, and that the way to learn to read words is to learn letters first. No one questioned this. Everyone agreed on the teaching method this conception suggested. . . . This logic dominated the teaching of reading until the reading process was studied in the psychological laboratory. The psychologists who became interested in reading about fifty years ago set out to determine how people actually read. They found that good

43

readers do not actually notice the letters or syllables that make up a word. The good reader takes in a whole word or phrase at a single glance, recognizing it by its outline. . . . Now we teach pupils to recognize short words as units from the very beginning. Sentences and short stories are introduced as soon as the pupil knows just a few words. Spelling-out and analysis of syllables used to be the beginning of instruction. Now they are taught later as reserve techniques, to be a "low gear" that the reader uses when he encounters a word that defies instant recognition.

Sounds very clear and convincing. In the horse-and-buggy age they taught the letters and sounds; then the men in white went to work in their laboratories and found something much superior; so now research has driven out the old-fashioned, prescientific procedure.

The trouble with this beautiful story is that it is wholly untrue. The word method was *not* adopted as a result of laboratory findings. Far from it. It started with a cow.

Before we get to that cow, let's look a little into the history of teaching reading. Let's begin at the beginning. What was the *original* method? How did those sixteenth-century free spellers become literate in the first place?

Well, in the beginning, school children were taught first the alphabet, then little syllables like *ab, ac, ad,* and then words, going from the simple to the more complex. Then they started reading the Bible. And that was that.

In colonial times in America, this system was incorporated in the famous *New England Primer,* the first American "best seller."

Then came Noah Webster. Webster, who was one of this country's great geniuses, made up his mind to replace the *New England Primer* with something better. In 1783, when he was twenty-five years old, he published his famous *Blue-Backed Speller,* which went into innumerable editions and was the universally used American primer for almost a hundred years. Eventually, an estimated hundred million copies were sold—

one of the most astounding figures in the whole history of printing and book making. The price was fourteen cents. Webster
supported his family with the income from his spelling book for
about twenty years, while he was working on his great dictionary.

What was the difference between the *New England Primer*
and Webster's *Blue-Backed Speller?* The difference was essentially that Webster was the first man who realized that an
English primer has to be based on phonetics. In his preface
he wrote:

Among the defects and absurdities found in books of this kind
hitherto published, we may rank the want of a thorough investiga-
tion of the sounds in the English language, and the powers of the
several letters—the promiscuous arrangement of words in the same
table. . . .
In attempting to correct these faults it was necessary to begin
with the elements of the language and explain the powers of the
letters.

And so Webster's book begins with an explanation of "the
powers of the letters"—what we would call today the elements
of phonetics or phonics. "Language is the expression of ideas by
articulate sounds. . . . Letters are the marks of sounds. . . .
Letters are of two kinds, vowels and consonants. A vowel is a
simple articulate sound formed without the help of another
letter, by opening the mouth in a particular manner, and
begun and completed with the same position of the organs. . . .
A consonant is a letter which has no sound, or an imperfect
one, without the help of a vowel. . . . A diphthong is a union
of two simple sounds uttered in one breath or articulation. . . ."

After that short preface begins the book—the book that was
used well into the second half of the nineteenth century to
teach American children to read—children in one-room school
houses, children on pioneer farms, children in log cabins that

contained no other books than the Bible and Webster's *Blue-Backed Speller*.

Was Webster's book primarily a reading book or a spelling book? The question cannot be answered. In Webster's time, reading and spelling were inseparable; nobody thought of teaching a child to read without teaching him or her to spell at the same time. The *Blue-Backed Speller* was a fourteen-cent medicine that cured you of illiteracy. Nobody dreamed of criticizing it as wrong, unscientific or ineffective.

But that doesn't mean that nobody tried to compete with that fabulously successful book. There were any number of other primers that tried to capture the market and failed. Among them, inevitably, were some that offered an entirely different approach—starting with whole words rather than individual letters. There was such a primer by Worcester in 1828 and another one by Bumsted in 1840. But the time hadn't come yet. The time came in 1846 when a young man named John Russell Webb published a primer called *The New Word Method,* which completely discarded the principle of "letters first" and was based on nothing but whole words.

And how did John Russell Webb arrive at his new method? Did he carry on tests and experiments? Did he utilize the results of research in psychological laboratories? Of course not. As I said before, it all started with a cow. In a later edition of Webb's primer, the story is told in complete—and highly plausible—detail:

The Origin of the Word Method

(The following brief history of the Word Method is published at the request of many friends of this system of teaching. Its author, Mr. Russell, is a nephew of the man after whom our author was named. —PUBLISHERS.)

On an early summer morning in 1846, a young man, barely twenty-one years of age, was reading a newspaper in the sitting-room of his boarding place. He was the teacher of the village school. From early boyhood he had been regarded as "odd." He did not do, he did not think, as boys of his age generally did. Often he was reproved for finding fault with what others considered "well enough." He would reply: "If we could see no defects, we would make no improvements." Many were the little devices, to save labor and give better results, seen on the home farm.

While awaiting breakfast, as already mentioned, a little girl, four or five years old, climbed into his lap as she had often climbed before. Her mother was in the kitchen preparing the breakfast; her father, in the yard milking the cow.

The teacher laid down his paper and began to talk to the child. The father was mentioned, what he was doing, and the cow was talked about. Just then his eye caught the word *cow,* on the paper he had laid down. He took it up and pointed out the word to the child, again calling attention to the cow, and to this word as the name of the animal her papa was milking. Soon she looked up into the teacher's face; her eyes kindled with intelligence; she caught the paper, jumped out of his lap and ran to her mother, exclaiming as she ran: "I know what it means; I know what it means. It is a cow, just like what papa is milking!" and she pointed out the word to her mother.

Many a boy and many a man before Newton had seen an apple fall. It may be that many a teacher had done just what this teacher did; but into him the circumstances had flashed an idea. He at once began to experiment, not only with the little four-year-old girl, but with the beginners in the school. The lessons were prepared in the evening, and in the morning printed on the blackboard, and he, himself, taught them to the children with the most marked—the most wonderful success. There were no unpleasant tones, no drawling. On the contrary, the children read in pleasant natural tones, giving the emphasis and inflections of the playground.

From time to time these lessons were printed and formed pages or hand cards. The children became very much interested in reading them. They read them in and out of school. They read them anywhere—everywhere one would listen. They took their cards with them to the table—to bed, as little girls sometimes do their dolls.

At first all the parents were very much pleased. But, alas! there was trouble ahead. It was soon discovered that the children could not spell the words—that they did not even know the names of the letters! Some of the parents "waited on the teacher," and left him with unpleasant memories. Others had faith that "That teacher knows what he is about." There was a good deal of talking, and what "the teacher" was doing became noised abroad.

That fall a Teachers' Institute was held at Watertown, twelve miles away. Our teacher was sent for. They wanted to know what the "new thing" was. For a week it was explained, illustrated, discussed. Then the following resolution was passed:

Resolved, That having heard an exposition of a new method of teaching children to read, by J. Russell Webb, we are of opinion, that the interests of our schools require its publication, and we pledge ourselves to use efforts to introduce its use into our schools should it be published.

Resolved, That a copy of this resolution be signed by our chairman and secretary and presented to Mr. Webb.

E. S. Barnes, *Chairman*
J. L. Montgomery, *Secretary*

Watertown, N.Y.
October 20, 1846

A Watertown bookseller (Joel Green) was present. He offered to publish an edition at his own expense—and he did, that fall, 1846. This edition bore the title: "John's First Book; or, The Child's First Reader."

The New York *School Journal* says: "That book was the means of a great reform. Millions of children have been saved years of drudgery by the use of the method it proposed, and Mr. Webb is entitled to unlimited praise."

And this is how the Word Method originated, and how it was born into the world. Since then it has written its own history.

Jay Russell

I don't doubt the truth of this charming story. After all, Mr. Jay Russell in 1855 had no earthly reason to make it up out of whole cloth. No, no, that's what happened: Twenty-one-year-old Mr. Webb ate his breakfast, the child climbed onto his lap, the cow was outside the window, and—lo and behold! —the word method was born. There was no new psychological theory, no years spent in the laboratory. It started with a cow.

And as soon as it did start, trouble started too—the kind of trouble that is still with us more than a hundred years later. Parents complained, the children didn't know the letters, and young Mr. Webb was exposed to some abuse. But he persisted —unfortunately—and *Webb's Normal Reader* was on its way —the first successful primer based on the word method.

Not that the word method immediately swept the field. Far from it. In those early years Webb's primer—like other primers based on the word method—was a novelty taken up only by experiment-minded teachers and schools. The phonetic method was still very much in the saddle and, as the word method gained ground, the phonetic method too became embroidered with all sorts of new experiments, like teaching children novel phonetic symbols, diacritical marks, and so forth. The word-method people replied that this sort of stuff was ridiculous— which it was—and proclaimed the blessings of the whole-word approach more loudly than ever.

Most American children, however, in the second half of the nineteenth century, were taught to read neither by the word method nor by the more extreme phonetic systems. They learned to read from Webster's Blue-Backed Speller and, after that fabulous best seller had finally run its course, they learned from the almost equally famous McGuffey Readers. As everybody knows, several generations of American children were brought up on the McGuffey Readers. And what system was used in McGuffey's primer? I went to the library and looked it up. Sure enough, it starts with letters and sounds.

After McGuffey—in the first quarter of the twentieth century—came several competing sets of readers, all firmly based on the phonic approach. Even those books and systems that favored the word method offered instruction in phonics too.

The idea of dropping phonics completely and relying solely on the "This-means-a-cow" approach still was far from anybody's mind. Around 1910 and 1920, the leading system was that used in the Beacon Readers, published by Ginn & Company in Boston—an efficient and intelligent sequence of systematic phonics, leading quickly to the reading of folk tales, fairy stories, and so on.

By the end of the 1920's, however, it was all over. No new phonic readers were published; Ginn & Company stopped revising the Beacon Readers, and finally *all* phonic readers went out of print. How come? For the answer to that question we must go back again—and this time to the psychologists.

The psychological theory back of the current way of teaching reading is very conveniently summarized in *The Psychology of Teaching Reading* by Irving H. Anderson and Walter F. Dearborn (Ronald Press, 1952). I quote from page 212:

Psychological Rationale of the Word Method

The psychological rationale of the word method has been demonstrated numerous times by laboratory studies of the psychology of reading. Cattell's study, reported in 1885, is a landmark. Using the tachistoscopic or short-exposure technique, Cattell found that the adult reader could, in ten minutes of exposure time, apprehend equally well three or four unrelated letters, two unrelated words (up to about 12 letters), or a short sentence of four words (or approximately 24 letters if in words). If the limit for unrelated letters was only three or four, the words obviously were not perceived in terms of letters. The experiment definitely proved that we do not ordinarily read by letters but by whole-word units.

Cattell's results were confirmed by Erdmann and Dodge in 1898. These workers found that the span for unrelated letters was only about four or five when a very brief exposure was used. Six or seven letters were often reported correctly when a longer exposure time was used, but that was about the limit for unrelated letters. Whereas familiar words, containing twelve to twenty letters, were easily read during an exposure time of 100 milliseconds.

These findings of Cattell and of Erdmann and Dodge delivered a damaging blow to the alphabet method and gave support to the movement already under way to revolutionize methods of teaching reading. The older notion had been that words are read by compounding the letters. That this is not the case was clearly demonstrated by the finding that words can be read when there was not time to grasp all the letters. Words must, therefore, be perceived in some other way. Cattell believed that the cue for recognition was the "total word picture," while Erdmann and Dodge used the expression "general word shape."

If we do not ordinarily read by spelling out the word or even by sounding it out in detail, little is gained by teaching the child his sounds and letters as a first step to reading. More rapid results are generally obtained by the direct method of simply showing the word to the child and telling him what it is.

I quoted this whole passage because it is extremely important to what I am talking about. Mind you, this is the sum total of the scientific basis for the word method as offered in the latest and most comprehensive book on the psychology of teaching reading. This is it; this is the whole psychological basis for the way your child is taught to read today—or, more exactly, trained to become a lifelong word guesser.

Let's look closely at what the psychologists are telling us here. They tested adult readers (*not* children) in a laboratory. They found that these adults could read letters that formed words faster than letters that did *not* form words. Therefore, they say, it is "obvious" and "clearly demonstrated" that readers don't read the letters that make up words but "perceive words in some other way." So—let's forget about teaching children the letters and simply tell them what the words mean.

You don't need to be a trained psychologist to see that this doesn't make sense. Naturally, a grown-up person who has been reading English for some thirty or fifty years has gotten used to the combinations of letters in common words. He does an extremely fast job of reading these familiar letter combinations, "compounding the letters" as automatically and unconsciously as he does everything else he has been doing for a lifetime. Does this mean that you can skip the whole process and teach a small child to perceive words in some mysterious "other way"? It does not. If you don't teach a child the letters, he'll always be stumped when he sees a new word.

In spite of what Anderson and Dearborn say in their book, this absurd theory was *not* very influential in the change-over from the phonic method to the word method. The primer writers and the classroom teachers at first did not much care for the fancy new theories—particularly since they flew in the face of all common sense. (A small minority, though, stuck to Webb's cow primers and similar ventures.) Things began to change in earnest only in 1908 when a man by the name of Dr. Edmund Burke Huey published a book called *The Psychology and Pedagogy of Reading*. Huey was a tremendously persuasive evangelist for the word method. He preached the new gospel as vigorously as nobody preached it before or since. For him, the word method was the dawn of a new world. Writing as if in a fever, he would raise himself to such incredible flights of fancy as this one:

Even if the child substitutes words of his own for some that are on the page, provided that those express the meaning, it is an encouraging sign that the reading has been real, and recognition of details will come as it is needed. The shock that such a statement will give to many a practical teacher of reading is but an accurate measure of the hold that a false ideal has taken of us, viz., that to read is to say just what is upon the page, instead of to *think,* each in his own way, the meaning that the page suggests. Inner saying there will doubtless always be, of some sort; but not a saying that is, especially in the early reading, exactly parallel to the forms upon the page. It may even be *necessary,* if the reader is to really tell what the page suggests, to tell it in words that are somewhat variant; for reading is always of the nature of translation and, to be truthful, must be free. Both the inner utterance and reading aloud are natural in the early years and are to be encouraged, but only when left thus free, to be dominated only by the purpose of getting and expressing meanings; and until the insidious thought of reading as word-pronouncing is well worked out of our heads, it is well to place the emphasis strongly where it really belongs, on reading as *thought-getting,* independently of expression.

This is the purest statement of the word method that I have seen anywhere—carried to almost insane lengths ("Reading, to be truthful, must be free of what is on the page"). It's persuasive all right, though, and Huey's book—written throughout in the same hectic tone—began to be read and talked about in teachers' colleges and schools of education. Here at last was an apostle who seriously suggested that phonics should be discarded altogether. It seemed unimaginable in those years that classroom teachers would ever actually do that—but still, here was someone who said loudly that it could be done and should be done.

And now the curtain rises on the last act of this long drawn-out drama. We are in the middle of the 1920's, and here is Dr. Arthur I. Gates, doing research in reading at Teachers College, Columbia University. Dr. Gates is a true believer in the whole-word method; what's more important, he is also filled with the fervent belief that systematic instruction in phonics is a pure, unadulterated evil that must be destroyed. At this point in history, the word method is in the ascendant, but most schools still haven't given up good old-fashioned phonic drills. So Dr. Gates tackles the problem by proposing something that will take the place of those drills. Of course we need phonics, he admits; by all means, he's all for it. But let's give children phonics in such a way that they hardly notice it; let's make it unobtrusive; let's sneak it in casually, while the children are paying attention to something else. Let's not teach them systematically that the letter *m* says mmmm and the letter *s* says ssss; let's teach them the sound of *m* while they are reading about a monkey and the sound of *s* when they get to the word *sit*.

And so the great idea of "intrinsic" or "incidental" phonics is born. Dr. Gates sets up an experiment: one first grade is taught by his new "incidental phonics," another first grade—the control group—is exposed to conventional phonic drills. After a few months, the two groups are tested. Hurrah! the new method has won. And Dr. Gates is on his way to drive phonics out of American schools.

As I am going to show in the next chapter, this Gates experiment was the only test ever made in which systematic phonics came out second best. I studied Dr. Gates' book, *New Methods in Primary Reading,* carefully to see how this result came about. Apparently there were several reasons: For one thing, of course, the fifty children (twenty-five in each of the two classes) were tested after only a few months of instruction; to really find out which system is better, tests should be made after two or three years, in third grade, or perhaps in sixth grade, or even at the end of high school. Only then will the difference between the two methods really show up. But even aside from that, let's consider the situation in the Gates experiment. On the one hand, there is "old-fashioned" phonics—the thing to be disproved; on the other hand, there is the brand-new method of "incidental" phonics. The teacher in the experimental class naturally had to pay special attention to this presumably casual aspect of her teaching; the "incidental" element for her was the main element, the thing she knew Dr. Gates was eager to prove to the world. No wonder she did a good job of it; her mind was on it—in complete contrast to the mind of an average teacher in a typical school today, who has been told over and over again that phonics is something hardly worth mentioning in class at all.

And on top of all that, there was a special joker in all the Gates experiments: every test was timed. What does that mean? It means this: You give a child, say, two minutes to read aloud a group of twenty words. If the child has been taught systematic phonics, he'll tackle each of these words letter by letter, sounding it out if necessary to make sure he reads the word that's actually there. Within the two minutes this first-grader may manage to read in this fashion eight of the twenty test words, each perfectly right. But a child who has been taught by the word method (plus "incidental" phonics) isn't concerned at all with getting the words right. He has been trained to guess, and guess he does. He races through all the twenty words, guessing wildly, and by pure chance combined with his memory of words he has "met," he guesses 50 per cent right. Result: The first child's score is eight, the second child's ten. I analyzed Dr. Gates' test scores, and found that they were all of this type. *New Methods in Primary Reading* is filled to the brim with these spurious statistics, "proving" Dr. Gates' case.

The book was published in 1928, but Dr. Gates summarized his findings in an article, which appeared in April, 1927, in the *Journal of Educational Psychology.* The article climaxed in the following sentence: "That it will be the part of wisdom to curtail the phonetic instruction in the first grade very greatly, is strongly implied; indeed it is not improbable that it should be eliminated entirely."

By the time the book came out more than a year later, Dr. Gates had apparently realized that he had gone too far. Page 102 of *New Methods in Primary Reading* simply says, "That it will be the part of wisdom to curtail the phonetic instruction in the first grade very greatly, is strongly implied"—leaving out the bland suggestion of throwing phonetics right into the ashcan. But the deed had already been done: every educator in the land who was interested in reading had read the article with its plain conclusion. Now it was at last official. Word had gone out from Teachers College, Columbia, that phonics was out. The hour of triumph for the word method had arrived.

From there on the great battle turned into just a mopping-up operation. Phonics had now been officially pushed up into second grade, and it was to be "incidental" instead of systematic. During the 1930's phonics drifted from second into third grade and finally out of the primary grades altogether, until it became something just barely good enough for remedial reading in fifth and sixth grade; and "incidental" phonics got "incidentaler" and "incidentaler" until nobody could notice any trace of it in an ordinary classroom. It became officially accepted in the literature on reading that phonics was nothing but a "reserve technique" in "word recognition," just one out of many methods of learning how to read—and the very poorest and last one at that. In 1949, Dr. David H. Russell of the University of California published a book, *Children Learn to Read,* in which he described "seven different ways to recognize new or partly known words." Here is his list:

1. The general pattern, or configuration, of the word
2. Special characteristics of the appearance of the word
3. Similarity to known words
4. Recognition of familiar parts in longer words
5. The use of picture clues
6. The use of context clues
7. Phonetic and structural analysis of the word

You see? Phonetics has become a tool to be used only after everything else has failed. The child is supposed to go through six different ways of guessing before he is allowed to try actual reading.

Dr. Gates, who in 1927 rather modestly proposed "incidental," second-grade phonics instead of systematic first-grade phonics, has long since gone the whole way and now treats phonics with complete contempt. In June, 1953, he wrote an "official" pamphlet on *Teaching Reading* for the National Education Association. Under the heading "Skill in Word Recognition" he lists the following "good technics": "Skill in observing the word as a whole; then, if necessary, quickly searching for major parts, such as component words; then, if

necessary, isolating and pronouncing syllables; then, if necessary, isolating easily sounded letters and familiar phonograms,
such as *th, ain,* etc. . . . and finally a shrewd knack of shifting
from one approach to another. . . ."

You will observe that according to this latest word from on
high, phonetics—aside from "easily sounded letters and familiar phonograms"—doesn't come into the business at all any
more. The child is not even supposed to fall back on phonics,
even "if necessary"—clearly because phonics has long ago
ceased to be taught.

For to understand fully what has happened, you have to
realize that since the 1920's we are not only without phonic
primers and readers; we are also without textbooks and courses
in teachers' colleges that include phonics; and consequently
we are now, in the 1950's, without elementary-school teachers
who know anything about phonics except that it is "outmoded."
The vast majority of our school children today has never heard
of the difference between a long and a short vowel; but there
are by now also thousands and thousands of elementary-school
teachers who couldn't tell you the difference either.

And what did happen in the field of reading since phonics
died in the 1920's and early 1930's? Let's bring the story up
to date. Naturally, after the great debate over phonics had died
down and the word method—or "sentence method" or "story
method"—was firmly in the saddle, the time had come for all
sorts of refinements and elaborations. I won't go into all of
those theories and fads, but two are worth mentioning. One is
the movement toward teaching fewer and fewer words. Once
it was accepted that children must learn to read, Chinese fashion, by memorizing words, the race was on for making the job
easier and easier and easier. Let's give the poor little tots only
four hundred words instead of six hundred in first grade; let's
further simplify the second-grade readers and the third-grade
readers and the sixth-grade books and the junior-high-school
books and the senior-high-school books—there is no end to

what can be accomplished by a ceaseless, determined campaign against all "unfamiliar" words. I'll have more to say about all this in a later chapter, but there is no doubt that the great game of vocabulary cutting has been the main idea of the reading "experts" for the past ten or fifteen years.

The other "great new theory" that blossomed in the 1930's was the teaching of silent reading. You don't hear much about this particular fad any more, but it's so typical of the upside-down logic of the educators that it ought to be mentioned here. Briefly, the idea is that a good adult reader reads silently, without moving his lips; a poor reader or a remedial reading case usually moves his lips and mutters. Ah! said the educators, there's the trouble. We have to teach children to read silently. Of course, anybody with a modicum of common sense knows that a beginner naturally reads aloud and that the habit of silent reading develops gradually, as reading becomes faster and smoother. But no, the educators insisted: Let's *start* with silent reading, and the whole trouble of "vocalizing" will never arise. And how do you stop a child from his natural tendency to read aloud? Like this (I am quoting from *Improvement of Reading* by Dr. Louella Cole, published in 1938):

The simplest method is to render the speech mechanism incapable of pronouncing words, even partially. A simple and effective means of bringing about this result is to have the child put two fingers into his mouth, using them to separate his upper and lower teeth and to hold down his tongue. Nobody can articulate words with his mouth hanging open. If the child, through force of habit, moves his jaws to articulate, he bites his fingers. With the tongue and the jaws both out of commission, there will be no pronunciation. Instead of his fingers a child may use his ruler or a large-sized eraser. The fingers are better than either wood or rubber, however, partly because the pupil is unwilling to bite them and partly because he always has them with him!

Another, if even less elegant procedure, is to let the child chew gum while he is reading. His speech mechanism is out of commission not because it is at rest but because it is doing something else. No one can pronounce words and chew gum simultaneously. Naturally, a pupil should not persist in these techniques until they become habits. They should be used only until the tendency to pronounce words has been broken.

As I said, the fad of "silent reading" seems to have subsided in recent years. I doubt whether any school in the country today follows Dr. Cole's brilliant suggestions on the use of fingers, pencils, erasers, and chewing gum. But that doesn't mean that common sense has returned to our schools.

Very recently, though, the pendulum began to swing in the other direction. Not that there is much change to be noticed in the classrooms, but the clamor of parents about their nonreading, nonspelling children seems to have gotten on some educators' nerves. A defensive note has crept into the educational journals whenever the word *phonics* is mentioned. Witness Dr. John J. DeBoer, editor of *Elementary English,* reviewing a book on *Emotional Difficulties in Reading* in February, 1954. "The book," writes Dr. DeBoer, "should serve as a powerful corrective for the view that the answer to most reading problems is 'more phonics.'" And Dr. Emmett A. Betts of Temple University, Philadelphia, in the January 1954 issue of *Education,* has this to say:

For the past 150 years, the phonics fad has come and gone. Right now, the fad has again taken over reading. While there is a need for improving the phonics programs through the teachers, it should be obvious that this one gimmick ·will not make much of a dent in the reading problem.

Quite a change in attitude between 1783 and 1954. In 1783 Noah Webster proclaimed that "it is necessary to begin with the elements of the language and explain the powers of the letters." Now we are told that phonics is just a gimmick.

Which wouldn't really matter if our children were taught to read. But they are not.

Chapter V

PHONICS vs. NO PHONICS

Thomas H. Huxley once described the scientific attitude like this: "Sit down before fact as a little child, be prepared to give up every preconceived notion, follow humbly wherever and to whatever abyss nature leads, or you shall learn nothing."

The attitude of our experts on reading is quite different. Their minds are filled with preconceived notions, they have an utter disregard for facts, and they are unwilling to learn anything.

I said in the last chapter that whenever the results of phonics and of the word method were compared by tests and experiments, phonics came out on top. (I tried to explain why Gates' experiments were an apparent exception.) Let me repeat that statement and amplify it: In every single research study ever made phonics was shown to be superior to the word method; conversely, there is not a single research study that shows the word method superior to phonics.

I know that this seems an unbelievable claim. Let me explain why I feel justified in making it. Every researcher in every field of science begins his work by surveying the previous research literature in the field. Consequently, almost all research reports are equipped with footnotes and bibliographical references that cover everything that has been done up to that point. A few hours in a library, working back from the latest studies in a given area, are therefore usually enough to check the sum total of research done to solve a given problem.

A few weeks ago I spent two days in the library of Teachers

College, Columbia University, tracking down every single reference to a study of "phonics vs. no phonics." I carefully read each one of those papers and monographs. Naturally, it is possible that some item or items in the bibliography have escaped me; but I honestly don't think so. I covered the ground as diligently as I possibly could, looking for scientific evidence *in favor* of the word method.

There was none.

In the books and pamphlets by the "experts" there are plenty of statements referring to those research studies. Usually the findings are called "contradictory." Sometimes a few stray statistics are quoted out of context; sometimes the actual findings are boldly misrepresented. The result is always the same: the preconceived notions are endlessly repeated, the true facts are concealed.

The true facts are these, in chronological order:

In 1913, Professor C. W. Valentine of the University of St. Andrews in Scotland published in the *Journal of Experimental Pedagogy* the results of a brilliant experiment. He had hit upon the idea of solving the "phonics vs. no phonics" problem by teaching his college students to read English words written *in Greek letters*. So he transcribed a passage from Robert Louis Stevenson in Greek letters and gave two groups of twenty-four students each two minutes to decipher it. One group had first been coached in the Greek alphabet, the other had been coached in recognizing the *whole words* in the Stevenson passage, as they looked in Greek letters. Result: Those who had learned the alphabet did 200 per cent better.

Professor Valentine then tried a similar experiment with eight-year-old children at the University Training School in Dundee. The result was the same. It all added up, he reported, to "a striking victory for the phonic method."

In 1916, Miss Lillian B. Currier, a teacher in the public school of Tilton, New Hampshire, wrote a paper called "Phonics or No Phonics?" for the *Elementary School Journal*.

(In 1923 she followed it up with another paper under the same title.) Miss Currier had taken two groups of children in first and second grade, and taught one group *with* phonics and the other *without* phonics. She had no statistics to offer but reported that the "non-phonic" children read with more expression and interest, but the "phonic" children were more careful and more accurate in reading the words that were on the page.

Next we come to a report by Mr. W. H. Winch, *Teaching Beginners to Read in England,* published in this country in 1925. Mr. Winch, a leading British educator, carried out a number of statistical experiments with children in first grade. (English children start going to school at five, so that they start to read at what is kindergarten age over here. I'll come back to that difference in Chapter 6.) There were two groups of children, one taught by the phonic method, the other by the "look-and-say" (that is, whole-word) method. After two months the children were given four tests. The look-and-say group scored 62.8, the phonic group 79.1. Mr. Winch summarized these results simply: "The phonic group has scored a complete victory."

Next study: In the *Elementary School Journal* of May, 1928, Elmer K. Sexton and John S. Herron report on "The Newark Phonics Experiment." Sexton and Herron tested a thousand school children in Newark, New Jersey. In spite of a rather confusing experimental setup, they concluded that the results favored instruction in phonics.

Next: In the October 1930 *Journal of Education Psychology* Raymond M. Mosher and Sidney M. Newhall report on "Phonic vs. Look-and-Say Training in Beginning Reading." Fifty children in New Haven, Connecticut, were taught by the word method and seventy-three children by the phonic method. The two groups were given ten tests. Eight of the ten tests favored phonics.

Now comes a very interesting story (from *New York State*

Education, October, 1930): Miss Helen R. Braem is Head Teacher at Letchworth Village, a state institution for mental defectives. The inmates of that institution are boys under sixteen with an I.Q. of from 30 to 75. Naturally they are very poor readers; they make very little progress at their school which, following the New York State Department of Education, uses the sight-reading (whole-word) method. One nice day Miss Braem hits upon the idea of giving those boys phonics. She digs up some phonic primers and readers and goes to work on an experiment, forming a "Sight Reading Group" and a "Phonic Group." The results are amazing. After one year she observes: "The Sight Reading Group had started reading for two years; the Phonic Group had started it for one year; yet the Sight Reading Group made three times the number of mistakes and took almost three times as long to read the same test." Now that Miss Braem has found the answer to her problem, she decides to help the poor "Sight Reading Group" who were the victims of the experiment. After three years of sight reading she gives them instruction in phonics. Another eight months go by and they have caught up with the boys who got phonics right from the start.

Next, 1931: In the *Peabody Journal of Education* Mr. S. C. Garrison and Miss Minnie Taylor Heard write of "An Experimental Study of the Value of Phonetics." They experimented with about one hundred school children in first and second grade; one half had phonics, the other half had none—or rather, they had the so-called "intrinsic" phonics invented a few years earlier by Professor Gates of Teachers College, Columbia University. At the end, there was a series of tests. Total result: The phonics group scored 58.5, the other group 55.5. Three points in favor of phonics. *And,* Garrison and Heard report, the phonics group was also considerably better in spelling.

Several years pass. Then Mr. Harry L. Tate publishes a paper on "The Influence of Phonics on Silent Reading in Grade I" (*Elementary School Journal,* July 1937). A group of thirty-six first-graders were taught by the look-and-say method, another group of thirty-seven children were given exactly the same instruction plus fifteen minutes each day of drill and practice in phonics. After two months they were given three tests. Two of the tests ("silent reading" and "paragraph reading") were tests of guessing rather than reading and the word-method children scored slightly better. The third test, however, was a test of "word recognition." In this test the score of the phonic group put them 4.6 months ahead of their "normal reading age," which means, according to Mr. Tate, that they scored *270 per cent better* than the word-method group. In other words, fifteen minutes of phonics for eight weeks had pushed them half a school year ahead of children taught by the usual method. Mr. Tate comments that this result is "overwhelming proof of a reliable finding" and adds: "Phonetic instruction and drill, as judged by the results of the Gates Primary Reading Test, Type 1, is far superior to the look-and-say method in developing the ability to recognize words."

Let's proceed to another study in a somewhat different setting. Sister M. Dorothy Browne, of St. Joseph's College, Adrian, Michigan, writes her doctor's dissertation on "Phonics as a Basis for Improvement in Reading" (Catholic University of America, 1938). How about using phonics for remedial reading? she says. Let's see what phonics can do for sixth-graders. So she gives a ten-minute phonic drill to 160 sixth-graders in six parochial schools in Chicago, Detroit, and Washington, D.C. Another 160 students form a control group with no phonic drill. After nine months the two groups are tested. The "reading age" of the control group is 154.9 (that is, the norm for a child of twelve years and eleven months), that of the phonic-drill group 162.73 (thirteen years and seven months). Ten-minutes-a-day of phonics for nine months has put them eight months of "reading age" ahead of their fellow students. On the basis of her findings, Sister M. Dorothy Browne comes to this conclusion: "The study of phonics is helpful not only

to the pupil who is deficient in reading, but is even more effective in stimulating the better reader to further growth."

And now we have arrived at 1939, the publication date of
the most extensive and conclusive study of them all. It is the
dissertation of Mr. Donald C. Agnew, taking his doctor's degree
at Duke University. Mr. Agnew sets out to settle the old con-
troversy once and for all. Those limited experiments with experimental and control groups of first-graders are inconclusive,
he feels. Let's take *all* the children in *all* the schools in a city,
he says, and find out where they stand at the end of third grade
when the effect of reading instruction can really be effectively
measured. So one spring he gives tests to all the third-graders in
all the schools in Raleigh, North Carolina. Before he does that,
he gives to all teachers who ever taught these children an elab-
orate questionnaire; from the answers he figures for each
teacher the exact degree to which she uses phonics in her
teaching. Then he works out the statistical relationship between the children's test scores and the amount of phonics
they presumably got from their teachers.

The results are a terrific disappointment. They hardly show
any differences. Mr. Agnew, in danger of not getting his Ph.D.
degree, goes home and ponders. What went wrong? He comes
to the conclusion that his basic assumption was wrong, namely,
that a little phonics would go a long way. After all, the super-
visors of the Raleigh schools are word-method people; they
frown on phonics, and there is not one among their teachers
who would dare to do a real job of phonics in her class. The
value of phonics can only be proven when it is taken seriously
and taught systematically.

Fortunately, there is the city of Durham, North Carolina,
whose superintendent of schools is a pro-phonics man. All
teachers in Durham schools have to teach phonics whether they
like it or not. So Mr. Agnew gives another series of tests to
some three hundred third-graders in Durham. *Their* teachers
have all been teaching more phonics than even the most

phonics-minded teacher in Raleigh. (Mr. Agnew has established that fact again with questionnaires.) Nothing could be more conclusive than a comparison of those third-grade test scores in Raleigh and Durham.

Here is the lineup of Mr. Agnew's average test results:

Name of Test	Score of Children in Raleigh (Word Method)	Score of Children in Durham (Phonics)
Gates A 4	63.31	79.50
Gates A 5	23.85	32.17
Gates B 2	18.11	29.29
Gates B 3	9.29	15.20
Word Pronunciation	53.15	70.17
Gates Type A	4.03	4.08
Gates Type B	4.18	4.18
Gates Type C	4.11	4.61
Gates Type D	4.15	4.38
Pressey Vocabulary	59.26	71.85
Eye-Voice Span	31.89	37.94

As you can see, the Durham children scored higher *in every one of these tests* (except Type B, where the scores were even). In addition, Mr. Agnew also gave then the "Gray Oral Reading Check Test," Set II and Set III. This is a test where the results are measured by the number of errors made in reading. On Set II, the Durham children made on the average 2.35 errors, the Raleigh children made 8.79. On Set III the Durham children made 7.05 errors, the Raleigh children 17.50. (The time scores on these tests showed that the phonics-trained Durham children took a little over a minute to read each set, while the little Raleigh word guessers took considerably less than one minute to make two to four times as many errors.)

Mr. Agnew's conclusions were clear and emphatic:

Should phonetic methods be employed in the teaching of primary reading? The answer to this question can be given only when the purposes for teaching primary reading have been agreed upon. If the basic purpose in the teaching of primary reading is the establishment of skills measured in this study (namely: independence in word recognition, ability to work out the sounds of new words, efficiency in word pronunciation, accuracy in oral reading, certain abilities in silent reading, and the ability to recognize a large vocabulary of written words), the investigations would support a policy of large amounts of phonic training. If, on the other hand, the purposes of teaching primary reading are concerned with "joy in reading," "social experience," "the pursuit of interests," etc., the investigations reported offer no data as to the usefulness of phonetic training.

I can fully understand Mr. Agnew's outburst of sarcasm, since I worked my way through the same literature. It's exactly as he says: If you want to teach children how to read, you need phonics; if you just want to make them feel good, you don't.

After Mr. Agnew's definitive study, research in "phonics vs. no phonics" came practically to an end. Not, of course, because his conclusive results had made further studies unnecessary— rather, I suppose, because later potential researchers realized that if the Durham-Raleigh results couldn't change the educators' minds, then obviously nothing could.

I have only one more item that will bring the story up to date.

In December, 1943, Dr. David H. Russell reported in the *Journal of Educational Research* a study of first- and second-grade children in Vancouver, British Columbia. There were sixty-one children who were given day-by-day phonic work on sounds and extra practice in handwriting; fifty-five other children were taught little or no phonics. At the end of the experiment both groups were given twelve different tests of reading and spelling. The phonics-trained group did better on every one of those twelve tests. "The table [of test results] clearly reveals," comments Dr. Russell, "that the early and rather direct type of instruction in the phonics group has a favorable influence on achievement in spelling and reading."

Ironically, this same Dr. Russell is the man whom I quoted in an earlier chapter as the author of *Children Learn to Read* (1949), one of the leading word-method texts. I can't offer any explanation for this astonishing reversal; but then, it's inexplicable anyway how all the high priests of the word method have managed to disregard and by-pass the unanimous findings of Valentine, Currier, Winch, Sexton and Herron, Mosher and Newhall, Braem, Garrison and Heard, Tate, Browne, Agnew, and Russell.

After all this, you possibly expect me now to recite the evidence *in favor* of the word method. But, as I said at the beginning of this chapter, there is none. The story as I told it here is complete; this is the sum total of all experiments ever made. I have left out nothing and I have misrepresented nothing— to the best of my ability as a researcher.

The record is perfectly clear. The facts have been available to anybody in the field for many years. Our "scientific" educators simply don't *want* to know the truth.

Chapter VI

TWO YEARS WASTED

If you are a mother and have a child in second or third grade who can't read and spell, you'll sooner or later go to the school and complain that your child isn't taught the letters and sounds. You'll then be told, one way or the other, that phonics is utterly out of date; just wait, and your boy or girl will suddenly catch on.

But if your child is in *first* grade, the answer you'll get will be considerably shorter, strongly resembling a brushoff. The teacher will tell you, with a rather indulgent smile: "He isn't ready, you know."

When you get to the subject of "readiness," you approach the holy of holies, the inner sanctum of the whole "science" of reading. In each of the fat tomes on how to teach reading, pages and pages are filled with profound discussions of what makes a child ready for reading, *when* does he get ready, how to tell whether he is or not, how to speed him up or slow him down, what to do with him before he gets ready, how to instill readiness, how to make it grow, how to use it, treat it, protect it, diagnose it, improve it, ripen it, and direct it. Deep mystery covers this whole recondite subject, and work has been going on for decades to explore its inner recesses.

One of the "authorities" in fact went so far as to devote a whole book to the subject of "reading readiness." I went through that whole book in search of a definition of "readiness," being sincerely curious to know what was meant by the word. But there was no definition to be found. So, since the experts don't seem able to help us, I'll offer my own definition. "Reading readiness" means the readiness of the *teacher* to let the child start reading.

If ever there was an example of reasoning in a vicious circle, this is it. You take a six-year-old child and start to teach him something. The child, as often happens, doesn't take to it at once. If you use a common-sense approach, you try again and again, exert a little patience, and after some time the child begins to learn. But if you are twentieth-century American educator, equipped with the theory of "readiness," you drop the whole matter instantly and wait until the child, on his own, *asks* to be taught. Let's wait until he's seven—until he's eight—until he's nine. We've all the time in the world; it would be a crime to teach a child who isn't "ready."

Some time ago, more or less by accident, I ran across what I'm sure is the first statement of the theory of "reading readiness." It's in Rousseau's *Émile,* the book that is the basis of all modern theories of education. This is how Jean Jacques Rousseau put the matter in 1762:

People make a great fuss about discovering the best way to teach children to read. They invent "bureaux" and cards, they turn the nursery into a printer's shop. [The French "bureau method" was a sort of anagram game by which French children were taught to read.] Locke would have them taught to read by means of dice. What a fine idea! And the pity of it! There is a better way than any of those, and one which is generally overlooked—it consists in the desire to learn. Arouse this desire in your scholar and have done with your "bureaux" and your dice—any method will serve.

Present interest, that is the motive power, the only motive power that takes us far and safely. Sometimes Émile receives notes of invitation from his father or mother, his relations or friends; he is invited to a dinner, a walk, a boating expedition, to see some public entertainment. These notes are short, clear, plain, and well written. Someone must read them to him, and he cannot always find anybody when wanted; no more consideration is shown to him than he himself showed to you yesterday. Time passes, the chance is lost. The note is read to him at last, but it is too late. Oh! if only he had known how to read! He receives other notes, so short, so interesting, he would like to try to read them. Sometimes he gets help, sometimes none. He does his best, and at last he makes out half the note; it is something about going tomorrow to drink cream —Where? With whom? He cannot tell—how hard he tries to make out the rest! I do not think Émile will need a "bureau." Shall I proceed to the teaching of writing? No, I am ashamed to toy with these trifles in a treatise on education.

I will just add a few words which contain a principle of great importance. It is this—What we are in no hurry to get is usually obtained with speed and certainty. I am pretty sure Émile will learn to read and write before he is ten, just because I care very little whether he can do so before he is fifteen. . . .

Now this, to be sure, makes a great deal of sense. Learning is most effective when there is strong motivation. If you are willing to wait five or ten years until a child is eager to read, then the teaching of reading will perhaps offer no problem.

But our educators, though in theory they are followers of Rousseau, would hardly say out loud that they would postpone the teaching of reading until the age of ten or fifteen. They know very well that people wouldn't stand for it. So, the next best thing, they use any device they can find to postpone the teaching of reading one, two, three years in the hope that by that time the child will be a little more eager to learn how to read. The most convenient of these devices is the theory that a six- or seven-year-old child is *unable* to learn how to read.

Please note that Rousseau didn't say any such thing in the passage I quoted. He obviously took it for granted that you *can* teach a small child to read, but simply said that he thought it better to wait. The idea that a six-year-old child *can't* learn to read is quite new, and a purely American invention.

To be quite fair, I should explain at this point that our

educators don't actually say that. They say—unanimously, as far as I can see—that a first-grader is able to grapple with some three or four hundred "sight words" and can memorize those in the course of one year. Then at the "mental age of seven" —that is, in second grade—he will develop "phonic readiness": he will be able to start learning a little something about letters and sounds. Phonics—*any* kind of phonics—before second grade is too much for a child, the educators say: they consider it an established fact that six-year-olds cannot learn phonics.

I have seen this statement repeated—and explained at length —in every single book on teaching reading that I have studied. The statement is always backed up by scientific evidence. There is always a footnote or bibliographical reference in those books when the subject of "phonic readiness" is discussed. The footnote is always the same. It refers to one single experimental study in which the onset of phonic readiness at seven was discovered. That study was made by Professor Edward W. Dolch of the University of Illinois and a graduate student of his, Miss Maurine Bloomster. It was published under the title "Phonic Readiness" in the November 1937 *Elementary School Journal.*

How did Professor Dolch and Miss Bloomster make their epochal discovery? You'd think it would be rather difficult to set up an experiment to prove that six-year-olds can't learn phonics, considering the fact that all over the world and through most of recorded history they have done just that. The only way to prove the point, logically, would be to do a bang-up job of teaching phonics in first grade, then give the children tests at the end of the year, and show, statistically, that phonics, with most of the children, "didn't take." In 1937, with the word method prevailing almost everywhere in the country, this would have meant going back to old-fashioned phonics and experimentally exposing a class of children to it for a year.

But Dr. Dolch didn't dream of doing anything like that. He experimented in a school where "phonics had had some emphasis, though not an unusual amount." Does that mean systematic phonics? It does not. It doesn't even mean "incidental" phonics. Dr. Dolch's experimental school—probably the University of Illinois Training School—was a school where phonics was something the children had to learn by themselves, if at all. "Phonics," in Dr. Dolch's meaning of the word, "means the use of generalizations . . . learned inductively. After the child has perceived that four or five words beginning with a certain sound begin with the same letter, he is supposed to have learned the generalization that all words beginning with that letter begin with the associated sound, and he is supposed to use this generalization in new word situations." Which makes it quite clear that the "not unusual amount of emphasis on phonics" in that school consisted in leaving the children completely to their own devices and teaching them no phonics whatever.

Having picked this school to test their theory of "phonic readiness," Dr. Dolch and Miss Bloomster proceeded to test how much the first- and second-graders knew of phonics. The tests were of the most primitive kind—the type of problem that a phonics primer presents on the first few pages. The children were given lines of four words like "cap nap tap lap" or "cap cape tap tape" or "lap clap slap flap," and were asked to tell the words apart. The first-graders—who had never been told anything at all about letters and sounds—turned out to be completely helpless; the second-graders managed to figure out a word here and there. Whereupon Dr. Dolch and Miss Bloomster announced to the world: "Children with mental age below seven made only chance scores; that is, as far as this experiment indicates, a mental age of seven years seems to be the lowest at which a child can be expected to use phonics."

And that, if you please, is all the scientific basis of the great discovery of "phonic readiness." First-graders can't take it, the educators tell us: see the report by Dolch and Bloomster in 1937.

The truth is, of course, that any normal six-year-old child *loves* to learn letters and sounds. He is fascinated by them. They are the greatest thing he's come up against in his life. He loves making noises; he loves taking things apart and seeing what they are made of. So here is a wonderful new game where you take words apart to learn what they are made of. And you learn how to make signs on paper that stand for certain sounds and noises. The child thinks this is the greatest invention ever made. (He's right in that.) He plays with this new toy endlessly. There are endless combinations of these sound-signs—and they make words, words that he knows and can recognize. He reads street signs—he writes words on every surface he can find—he works out sentences in the newspaper —finally he reads a book. Motivation? Rousseau was wrong when he relied on the necessity to get information. A normal child is ready and eager to learn to read because it's mankind's most fascinating game.

But then, you will say, what's the explanation of the obvious fact that our first-graders don't get on with their reading— that they often show hardly any interest in it—that they take years before they "discover" books, if they ever do it at all? My answer to this is again the difference between phonics and the word method. Start a child with letters and sounds, make him understand the basic principle underlying all alphabetic writing and reading—and pretty soon he will be on his way, having discovered that reading is fun. But start a child for a year, two years, three years with the senseless, stultifying activity of staring at a collection of letters memorizing that it means "chicken" or "funny" or "walked," and he'll never develop the slightest interest in reading. Why should he? The fun in reading lies in the great game of deciphering a hidden mean- ing—just as the fun in writing lies basically in the game of encoding a message. With our system, it is many years before the child even realizes that this is what the game is about.

Mr. Winch, the British schoolmaster whose book on *Teach-*

ing Beginners to Read in England I quoted in the last chapter, had some wise things to say on this point: "The argument for the look-and-say method is tainted by the limited-adult view of the child-mind. Our own psychological processes are put into the child, diminished in strength, but similar in form. We are getting old and worn, many of us. We do not like the mechanical acquisition of new things; it is hard for us; so we say children do not like it. As a matter of fact, they do. Repetition bores us; so we say it bores the young child. As a matter of fact, he loves it."

Exactly. The real reason for the horrible fiasco of the word method is that it looks at a child as if it were a small-size adult. So the child is forced, by hook or crook, to grasp words as wholes like an experienced grown-up reader, to read silently without moving his lips, to act as if it were a shame to play with words and letters and sounds. To an adult, the ABC is something childish; so the child is taught to refrain from such childish habits and to concentrate on reading as "thought-getting." He is praised and rewarded if, after weeks and months, he has learned to say "dog" while looking at the letter combination "d-o-g"; but he is never once given the opportunity to look at a brand-new word like, say, "fib," to slowly decipher it by sounding it out, and then to repeat happily, with a tremendous sense of achievement: "Fib, fib, fib, fib, fib, fib!! It means fib! It means fib!"

Six-year-olds can do that. They are doing it, today, at the very moment that you are reading these words, in Germany, in France, in Norway, in Spain, in South America—all over the civilized world. The problem of "reading readiness" or "phonic readiness" has never for a moment troubled any of the inhabitants of those countries. They decided, long ago, that in order to educate their children, they had to start them on the Three R's at six. So, all over the world, reading starts at the age of six.

Except—and this may shock you—in Great Britain, where it

starts at the age of five. Yes, it's an old, time-honored British custom to teach five-year-olds to read.

When I discovered this fact in Mr. Winch's book, it was news to me. So I checked and made sure that it was true—and is still true today. The information I got was perfectly clear: Reading in England starts in the first year of Infant School, and Infant School starts at the age of five. There are two years of Infant School, covering what is here kindergarten and first grade. Then come four years of Junior School, beginning at the age of seven, what is here second-grade age. Reading and writing, I repeat, start at the age of five.

Why do the English do that? Why do they start their children a year earlier than is customary on the European Continent? I have never seen an explanation anywhere, but I think the answer must lie in the wretched system of English spelling. Most European languages are reasonably phonetic in their spelling, but English, as we have seen, is saddled with 13 per cent irregularly spelled words.

Probably any other nation in the world would have reformed its spelling under these circumstances. But the English are not like that; if the whole world has decimal units of currency, they hang on to their pounds and shillings and pence. If English spelling adds a year to the job of learning how to read and write, why, then English children have to start when they are five. Very simple solution, really. By the time they are six or seven, they'll be just as far advanced as children in Germany and France.

And so we have the ages of schooling pretty well standardized all over the world, with school beginning at six in most countries, except in Great Britain where it starts at five. Achievement in the grades and at high school and college age is pretty much the same the world over.

In the United States the picture is entirely different. Generally speaking, students in our schools are about two years behind students of the same age in other countries. This is not a wild accusation of the American educational system; it is an established, generally known fact. I know of innumerable cases of young Austrians and Germans who applied for admission to college or university in this country. The standard practice is to give those students credit for two years of college if they have finished what corresponds to our high school abroad. And that rule of thumb works: if you assume that a foreign student is about two years ahead of an American his age, you are usually just about right.

What accounts for these two years? Usually the assumption seems to be that in other countries children and adolescents are forced to study harder. Now that I have looked into this matter of reading, I think the explanation is much simpler and more reasonable: Americans take two years longer to learn how to read—and reading, of course, is the basis for achievement in all other subjects. One of those two lost years is the year they lose by starting at six instead of, like the English, at five. The other is the year lost through using the word method instead of phonics.

Let's look at it this way: English spelling takes about a year longer to learn than the spelling of most other languages. The British recapture that lost year by starting to learn a year earlier. But the American attitude is entirely different. If English spelling makes it hard to learn how to read, let's do the job some other way. Let's invent a new gadget by which we can teach reading without teaching the letters at all. If the word method takes a year longer and is only half as effective—so what? This is the richest country in the world; we can afford it. Let's not think of spoiling the happy year in kindergarten with teaching reading; and let's shield our children from the dangers and confusions of English spelling by giving them a substitute way of reading whole words. And so, what takes one year in the rest of the world and two years in England takes at least three years here. At twelve, American children know as much as other children at ten; at twenty, they are matched with foreign eighteen-year-olds.

As I said, it's the typical American attitude that we can afford this tremendous waste of our resources. We treat those two years in the lives of our children as we treat our soil, our timber, our oil. Perhaps we can. But at least we should realize what we are doing. We take two years, which we could save by starting with phonics at the age of five, and spend them on games, toys, and coloring books.

If our educators are really in favor of this system, they should say so. But they shouldn't insult our intelligence and that of our children by brandishing the word "readiness" as if it had any real meaning.

Chapter VII

"OH, OH! COME, COME! LOOK, LOOK!"

The other day I attended a meeting at our local school at which parents discussed reading problems with the school librarian and the remedial reading teacher. One of the mothers stood up and made an interesting point. "Why is it," she asked the librarian, "that my two boys, who are in first and second grade, never bring home any library books that they can read themselves? My husband and I have to read those books to them. Can't you give them books that they can read themselves?"

There wasn't much the librarian could say in answer to that question. She just didn't have any such books in her library, she said. Publishers didn't put out any books simple enough for first- and second-graders to read alone. Sorry, but the lady and her husband would just have to go on reading aloud to their boys.

All of which was perfectly true. What was also true, but what of course nobody said, was that first- and second-graders in our public schools are not taught to read at all, as shown by the fact that there isn't a single book on the market that they can manage to read by themselves. Instead, they are taught to memorize the words contained in their readers.

To understand what exactly is happening in our schools, it is necessary to understand clearly what those readers are, how they are produced, and what effect they have on our children. Let's look at them in some detail.

To begin with, you have to realize that what is now commonly known as a reader is not at all the kind of thing a reader used to be thirty or forty years ago. In those days a reader was simply a collection of reading matter suitable for children in school. Today a reader is something entirely different. It is a special tool for fixing a "sight reading vocabulary" in children's minds. This "sight reading vocabulary" is the essence of the word method of teaching reading. The word method therefore hinges on the use of those readers. Without the readers, the word method cannot be used at all.

According to the basic theory of the word method, children learn to read by looking at words again and again until they know them by sight. It is therefore necessary to make them fix their eyes repeatedly on certain predetermined words. For example, during first grade a reading "expert" decides to give them, say, four hundred words. He draws up a list of those four hundred words and then proceeds to write a book of "stories" containing no word outside that list and repeating each one of the four hundred words as often as possible. He then repeats the process for the second-grade reader of his series: he adds another four hundred words to the first four hundred, draws up a list of those eight hundred words, and writes a somewhat fatter book of "stories" staying within his eight-hundred-word limit and repeating each of the eight hundred words to the utmost. Now he goes on to his third reader. Another four hundred words are added; the list now contains twelve hundred words; the book is again a little fatter and now contains the maximum variations upon the twelve hundred words. The "expert" proceeds in the same manner with his fourth reader, his fifth reader, and his sixth reader, and winds up with a package suitable for handsome annual sales.

Naturally, the word lists differ to some extent from one set of readers to another. The sets put out by the various publishers are therefore not interchangeable. If a child has mastered the second-grade reader of the Scott, Foresman set, that doesn't mean at all that he is now ready for the Third Reader of the Macmillan set. All it means is that he supposedly is able to recognize the eight hundred or nine hundred Scott, Foresman words when he sees them.

At this point you may possibly doubt the accuracy of my figures. Let me therefore say right here that I checked the vocabulary contents of the two leading sets of readers, Scott, Foresman Company and Macmillan Company. (This proved to be a very easy research job since all elementary textbook houses proudly include vocabulary statistics in all their readers.) The Scott, Foresman set includes 1,280 words in the first two grades and adds 498 in third grade, reaching the grand total of 1,778 words at the end of third grade. The Macmillan Company, however, is ahead of the game by a considerable margin. The latest edition of their set of readers is pared down to not more than 1,284 words by the end of third grade.

I don't want to bore you with more of these vocabulary figures, but it is important to add that the trend is definitely toward fewer and fewer words. A sharply limited vocabulary seems to be the most potent sales argument for school readers, and since the competition is extremely keen, the figures get lower from year to year.

The effect of this in the classroom is best described in the words of Professor Gertrude Hildreth of Brooklyn College, author of *Teaching the Three R's,* who seems to be one of the pioneers in the great vocabulary-cutting movement. Professor Hildreth is the senior author of a set of readers that gets along with 1,147 words for the first three grades. "Experience has proved," Dr. Hildreth writes, "that keeping the vocabulary of new words relatively small—even a little below the children's demonstrated assimilation threshold—without neglecting the other important factors, virtually revolutionizes the teaching of primary-grade reading. A teacher in a southern state reports that the use of books with simplified vocabulary has cut down reading difficulties in the first three grades by 75 per cent. Second and third grade teachers, particularly, find the teaching of

reading a joy instead of a chore when word difficulties are re-
duced."

In other words, teaching children 1,147 words in three years
is a cinch. Never mind the fact that those third-graders can't
read a single blessed book and are unable to decipher a simple
note to the milkman—what does it matter as long as the teacher's work is now a joy instead of a chore?

Possibly, however, these figures don't look as ridiculous to you
as they actually are. How many words *should* a child know when
he has reached the end of third grade?

To answer that question, I must point out to you that the
question itself is meaningless when you teach reading by the
phonic method. In that case, you take about two years to give
the child such a thorough knowledge of letters and sounds that
he can read virtually anything. Then, if you want to, you take
a third year for review, making 100 per cent sure that the child
knows all the important phonic principles and exceptions. So
your third-grader will be able to read whatever interests him,
whether the vocabulary range is 1,200 words or 5,000 words or
40,000 words. The vocabulary range of the reading material he
can master will therefore depend not on the number of "sight"
words he has learned—he hasn't learned words, he has learned
how to read—but on the number of words he knows *by sound*.
That number, according to the researches of the late Dr. Seashore of Northwestern University, is astonishingly high. It is,
for a third-grader, 44,000 words.

You may not believe this figure, of course—although it was
arrived at scientifically by sampling a large unabridged dictionary and asking children whether they could define the
words. However, maybe the figure is too large. Maybe the average third-grader's vocabulary is only 34,000 or 24,000 or even
14,000. Whatever it is, there is not the slightest doubt that it is
at least ten times as large as the number of words he learned to
read in school by any of the methods now in use. After three
years of "learning to read" he is totally unable to decipher 90
per cent of his own speaking and listening vocabulary when he

sees it in print. No wonder the library has no books he can take home and read.

And now let's take a look at what's in those books. Don't underrate their importance in the life of your child. They are all he has to read—all he *can* read—during the first two or three or four years that he comes in contact with books. For all he knows, this is what books are like. The grownups insist that reading books is a terribly important thing; as far as he knows, this means that there is something almost magically significant in saying aloud the words printed in his readers.

Here, for example, is the full text of a "story" called "A Funny Ride," taken from the Scott, Foresman First Reader, *Fun With Dick and Jane*:*

Father said, "I want something. I want to get something. Something for the car. We can get it here."

"Oh, Father," said Sally. "What do you want? What do you want for the car?"

Father said, "You will see. You will see."

Up, up went the car. "Oh, oh," said Jane. "See the car go up. The car can go for a ride. It can ride up."

Sally said, "Oh! See Tim! He went up, too. He and Spot and Puff went up."

Sally said. "Look, Father! Spot and Puff want to jump. Please make the car come down. Can you make it come down?"

"Yes, Sally," said Father. "We can make the car come down. We will get Spot and Puff and Tim."

"Look, Sally," said Dick. "See the car come down. See Tim come down. See Spot and Puff come down."

Sally said, "Down comes the car. Down comes Spot. Down comes Puff. And down comes Tim."

"Oh, Spot," laughed Dick. "You ride up. You ride down. You ride up and down. This is a funny ride for you. A funny ride for Puff. And a funny ride for Tim."

Father went to the car. He said, "The car can go. The family can go. The family can go away."

---

* From *Fun With Dick and Jane* by Gray and Arbuthnot. Copyright 1940 by Scott, Foresman and Company, and used with their permission.

"Away we go," said Sally. "We will not ride up and down. We will ride away." Away went the car. Away went the family. Away, away, away.

I hope you see from this why I always put the word "stories" in quotation marks in this chapter. These little somethings are *not* stories. They are artificial sequences of words—meaningless, stupid, totally uninteresting to a six-year-old child or anyone else. Without the pictures they are even unintelligible. In this case, the family stops at a gas station and the car is jacked up with the dog, the kitten and the teddy bear in it. But the "story" doesn't say so. It concentrates mainly on the repetitious babble of three-year-old Sally.

What is it that makes this "story" so extraordinarily inane and gives it its peculiar, vaguely feeble-minded flavor? To answer that, let me analyze the vocabulary. There are altogether 239 running words of text here, but only 47 *different* words. This means that 80 per cent of all the words are repeated words. The clue to understanding what is happening here lies in the element of repetition.

Imagine yourself for a moment in the position of one of the educational drudges assigned to the job of concocting one of those readers. You have, say, four hundred words to work with. You have to fill a book with "stories." That means that each word has to be repeated, say, an average of twenty-six times. How is this to be done? The only possible way to accomplish that result is to repeat, repeat, repeat words, phrases, sentences endlessly. "Oh, oh! Come, come! Look, look! You will see. You will see. See the car come down. See Tim come down. See Spot and Puff come down. Away went the car. Away went the family. Away, away, away."

This sort of strung-out prose has no resemblance any more to normal English. It is word-method-reader idiom, a language to be found solely and exclusively in the books manufactured for use with and on American school children. It is *not* the language used in telling a story, making a narrative interesting, or conveying information intelligibly. No normal writer ever wrote a book like that, no poet ever wrote such a poem, no mother ever told such a bedtime story. Our literature is composed in English, *not* in "Oh, oh! Come, come! Look, look!" language.

For a comparison of this language with standard English I took the story of the three little pigs, as printed in *It Happened One Day,* the Supplementary Second Reader in the "Alice and Jerry Books" series (Row, Peterson & Company, Evanston, Illinois). In this version the story has 1,243 words and begins as follows:

Once upon a time there was an old mother pig. She had three little pigs.

The three little pigs ate and ate. Then they danced and sang.

The mother pig and the three little pigs lived in one house.

The three little pigs grew and grew. They grew so big that they could not all get into the house.

One day the old mother pig called the three little pigs.

She said, "You are too big and fat to live in this house. You must each have a house of your own."

"Where will we get so many houses?" said the three little pigs.

"You must build them," said the old mother pig. "You must each build a good house. Then the wolf can not catch you."

Now, the three pigs did not want to work. They did not want to build houses.

They danced and sang and did not do as their mother said. Then the old mother pig was angry.

She called the three little pigs to her and said, "You must each build a house. You must build it right away. Then the big bad wolf can not catch you."

So the three little pigs went away to build the houses.

There are 204 running words in this opening passage and 76 *different* words, which means that 63 per cent of the words are repeated words. (Not as high a percentage as in our first-grade example, but still fantastically high.)

Now let's look at a normal English version of "The Three Little Pigs." This version, containing exactly the same story, gets along with 583 words, as against 1,243 in the word-method-reader version. The corresponding opening passage reads here as follows:

An old mother pig and her three little pigs lived in a very small house.

One day Old Mother Pig said, "This house is too small for us. Little pigs, you must go away. You must each make a house."

So the first little pig went away to make a house.

In this straightforward version with its classic economy of words, there are 51 words and 35 *different* words. The rate of repetition is 31 per cent.

If you want to, you can make this experiment yourself on any kind of writing that happens to be handy. You will find that the normal ratio is about one repeated word to two new ones. A ratio of one new word to two repeated words is highly abnormal. The effect is tiresome and soporific to the extreme. Such a language is *not* "simplified English" or "children's English" or "easily readable English" or any kind of English that can be read with interest and enjoyment. It is *diluted* English, one part English and one part added repetition.

And now let me explain where I found the original version of "The Three Little Pigs." It appears in Book Two of the Beacon Readers, published by Ginn and Company Ltd. in England. As you may remember from an earlier chapter, the Beacon Readers used to be the leading set of phonic readers in this country until the word-method partisans forced them off the market. Well, those same Beacon Readers, twenty-five years out of print in this country, are still going strong in England; in fact, they are the most widely used set of readers over there. I studied those English Beacon Readers. The basic principles are still exactly the same as those of the old American Beacon Readers. There is a little more sight reading now in the first few weeks or months; but after that phonics is presented as fully and systematically as in any material that I have seen.

"The Three Little Pigs"—and this is the most significant point of my comparison—appears, as I have said, in Book Two of the Beacon Readers. Book Two is scheduled to be read at the end of the first year of learning how to read, that is, *the first year of Infant School*. Which means that English children, trained by phonics, read "The Three Little Pigs" at kindergarten age, when they are five.

And where did I find "The Three Little Pigs" in the Row, Peterson series? I found it in a Supplementary Reader for use in second grade. "The Three Little Pigs," in their diluted version, are here considered second-grade material, to be read two years later than in England, at the age of seven.

Of course I talked about that two-year difference in the last chapter. But what I want to point out here is how it works out in actual practice. In England, where the relationship between age and reading ability is normal and undistorted, five-year-olds are able to read nursery tales. They are able to read the material that is natural for their age. The same is true for six-year-olds, for seven-year-olds, and so on. The problem of specially simplified materials for school children doesn't exist. When children are mentally ready for fairy tales, they can read fairy tales; when they are ready for Sir Walter Scott, they can read Scott; when they are ready for Dickens, they can read Dickens.

In fact, the authors of the Beacon Readers found that with their phonic method they ran into the opposite problem of finding material that is interesting to children and *challenging enough* for their advanced skill in reading. I quote from the preface of Book Four of the Beacon Readers: "A thorough mastery of phonetic principles gives the child such power over new words that it is difficult to find enough reading material properly graded from a phonetic point of view to satisfy his needs."

To read this today, in the United States of the 1950's, makes you almost weep. We have long since reached the point where we reduce not only the vocabulary of all readers in the first six grades, but also the vocabulary of all textbooks in other subjects, of junior-high-school books, of senior-high-school books, and now even of some college texts. Everybody today accepts it as gospel that all books for children and adolescents have to be thinned, watered, diluted. We do not dare any more to expose our children to normal English.

Which means, as I pointed out before, that the vast majority of our children are unable to read Andersen's *Fairy Tales* and *The Arabian Nights* and Mark Twain and Louisa May Alcott and Robert Louis Stevenson and Edgar Allan Poe and Charles Dickens and Conan Doyle *at the age where they would truly enjoy those books*. They may reach the point where they can read those books two or three years later than an English child —but then it's too late. The golden hour has passed when *Treasure Island* really means what it should mean to a boy. No. The sad fact is that the word method has alienated most of our children from the books that English-speaking children and adolescents have read and enjoyed for many generations. This is an irreparable damage. It may be possible to restore sanity in the field of reading and return to the teaching of reading rather than word guessing. But it will never be possible to bring back to adolescents and adults the lost hours of magic childhood reading—and rekindle in them emotions they have never felt.

Chapter VIII

HOW NOT TO TEACH READING

And now let's have a look at what actually happens in the classroom. Come with me and visit a typical American school.

Let's go down the street to the public school. It's an ordinary Monday morning early in March. The time is 9 A.M. Let's walk into a first-grade room.

There are about twenty-five children in this class. Their teacher is a bright young woman, not too long out of teachers' college, who takes her job seriously.

The children are divided into three groups when it comes to reading—the upper group, the middle group, and the lower group. In this particular class the three groups are about equal in size, it so happens. Of course the children are not told that they are grouped according to their ability; but children always know these things by instinct anyway.

The reading period consists in the teacher calling each of the three groups to assemble on their little chairs around her in front of the room, while the other two-thirds of the class do something else—drawing, it seems, or writing in their workbooks, or nothing in particular. Meanwhile, the reading group performs for about ten or fifteen minutes. The teacher asks them to open their books ("Where were we?") and they start, one after the other, going around the circle. First Tom reads a few lines, laboriously following the words with his finger, then Barbara, then Dick, then Sandra, then Joe, then George, then Louise, then Mary.

Tom reads: "Jack ... Ran ... Out ... To ... See ... The ... Truck ... It ... Was ... Red ... And ... It ... Was ... Big ... Very ... Very ... Big ..."

"Barbara?" says the teacher.

"It ... Had ... Come ... To ... Take ... Jack ... Far ... Away ... To ... His ... New ... Home ... Far ... Away ... To ... His ... New ... Home ... On ... A ... Big ... Farm ..."

This is the end of the page. The teacher turns to Dick. "Dick?"

Dick starts again at the top: "Jack ... Ran ... Out ... To ... See ... The ... Truck ..."

This is the pattern, repeated day after day. They "read" from their little readers, in small groups, one page at a time, several times over. They do not read a story from beginning to end, as it was so neatly planned in the schools of education and in the publishers' offices. They read two, three, four pages, if that, starting from wherever they left off last Friday and ending after fifteen minutes to make room for the next group. As to the performance of the three groups, it's pretty much the same. The top group is a few pages ahead of the second group in the First Reader, and the lowest group is still struggling through the preceding primer.

But the thing that is so characteristic, the unforgettable hallmark of American instruction in reading, is the *way* they "read." It's a sort of chant, one word at a time, each produced with the same monotone and heavy effort. Tom and Barbara and Dick and Sandra know that they are supposed to say certain words while their fingers move from one group of letters to the next. There is one word out of some forty or fifty that is right and all the others are wrong. The game consists in hitting the word that the teacher says is right.

It is obviously ridiculous to assume that these children "read" the "stories" in any acceptable meaning of the words. There is hardly any story to begin with, and whatever there is, is fully shown by the picture on the page they are looking at, in addition to its having been told and explained at length by the teacher beforehand. Then they "read"—one, two, three, four times the same few sentences on the page. If the words on the page had any novelty at all for Tom and Barbara, they certainly don't have any freshness whatever for the other six.

Anyway, they *don't* read. Just listen to them: "The . . . Moving . . . Men . . . Jumped . . . Down . . . From . . . The . . . Truck . . They . . . Went . . . Right . . . Into . . . The . . . House . . . They . . ."

Of course they make mistakes. That is to be expected, since they are learning. But perhaps you are still not prepared for the *kind* of mistakes they make. One girl reads "said" instead of "jumped" with full conviction that "said" is the right word. The next child is stumped by the word "truck" and simply stops, completely helpless. Little Jimmy, in the "middle group," reads "I" for "It." The teacher asks him to read the word again. He again reads "I." The teacher reminds him that "We had this word long ago, don't you remember?" But he *doesn't* remember; this is a Monday morning in March and maybe "we had the word" in January and he didn't pay any attention at the time. He thinks. Characteristically, he doesn't look at the word in the book, but stares into space, trying to revive the dim memory of a morning many weeks ago. Finally he says "At." He is told that this is wrong and that the word is "It." The reading proceeds. "It . . . Had . . . Come . . . To . . . Take . . ."

Finally, we watch the poorest group. They work on some "story" about a boy who is terribly excited and happy because he has two new caps, a blue one and a brown one. The teacher tries her best, in her preliminary telling of the story, to get the children interested. Unfortunately, they are not. The business of the two new caps leaves them utterly cold.

The teacher, following the golden words of the publisher's manual to the letter, puts the new words in the story on the blackboard. There are four new words, and the children are

given a little drill in telling them apart. Some are able to
do it, some aren't. One boy, confronted with the two words
"caps" and "houses" and asked to tell which is "caps,"
promptly points to "houses."

When they come to the sentence "I have two new caps" in
the book, another boy just stops, completely floored by the
problem. There is some discussion. Finally the teacher asks
the boy what *he* would say if his father had bought him two
new caps. The boy thinks. Then his face lights up. *Now* he
knows what the sentence says: "I got two new hats."

Let's walk into another first grade. There is not too much
difference. The teacher is a little younger, the atmosphere is
a little more relaxed, and the noise made by the nonreading
two-thirds of the class is considerably bigger. But the three
groups are there, and the succession of children's voices, and
the chant. "One . . . Morning . . . Alice . . . Was . . .
Playing . . . With . . . Betsy . . . Lee . . . Betsy . . . Lee . . .
Was . . . Alice's . . . Doll . . . Alice . . . Heard . . . Mother
. . . Call . . . She . . . Jumped . . . Up . . ."

But little Peter in the poorest group *doesn't* start with
"One morning Alice." He puts his finger under the first word
and begins "One . . . Two . . . Three . . ." The teacher
tries to explain to Peter that he has made a mistake. It *isn't*
"One two three." It is "One morning Alice." Peter obediently
repeats: "One . . . morning . . . Alice . . ."

In the best group they are on page 53. "Jerry . . . Look . . ."
"No, it isn't *look*. What's that word, Charlie?" "Jerry . . .
took . . ." "*That's* right. The word is *took*." "Jerry . . . Took
. . . Him . . . To . . . The . . . To . . . The . . ." "What's
the next word, Charlie? *You* know that word, don't you? We've
had it several times." Charlie can't remember. Peggy raises her
hand and says: "Pet." Charlie continues: "To . . . The . . .
Pet . . ." He doesn't know the next word either. The teacher
asks him to look at it. The word is *show*. Charlie looks at it,
then searches his memory. "Fish?" he says.

Judy is next. "The . . . Man . . . At . . . The . . . Show . . ." Judy relapses into silence. The next word is *chose*. "Oh yes," says the teacher. "You were out with the measles when we had that word two weeks ago. It's *chose*." Judy repeats "chose" and goes on.

Let's walk across the hall and look in on a third grade. Now that we have seen how the system starts in first grade, let's see the results. In third grade, supposedly, children are *reading*.

As we enter the third grade, we find that what goes on here is surprisingly similar to the work in the first grade. Again there are the three groups, the fifteen minutes per group, the chant. They cover more pages now, and they are a little surer of some of the words. But their mistakes are still of the same kind; if they don't know a word, they stop or they say an entirely different one.

The spread between the three groups has widened considerably. The top group is in the second half of their Third Reader, the middle group is way behind in the same book, the lowest group is in the middle of something called a "Readiness Third Reader."

We ask the teacher—a very pleasant, middle-aged woman—whether there is any child who is particularly outstanding in reading. Yes, would we like to listen to Gerald? He is really good, and he will read to us out of a volume of Andersen's *Fairy Tales* that happens to be handy. So we listen to Gerald. Gerald *is* good; in fact, he seems almost miraculous to us at this point. He reads words like *sentry* and *aristocratic* and pronounces them correctly, although it then turns out that he doesn't know their meaning. How come? we ask. It turns out that Gerald is "new." He is *not* a product of this school.

Meanwhile, the six or seven "poorest" readers have assembled in their little circle and the chant begins. "But . . . Miss . . . Lizzie . . . Was . . . Not . . . Afraid . . . Of . . . Any . . . Farmer . . . She . . . Shook . . . Her . . . Head . . . Faster . . . And . . . Faster . . ."

End of the page. Harry is asked to start again from the top. "I . . . Am . . . As . . . Sure . . . As . . . I . . . Stand . . . Here . . . That . . . Your . . . Dog . . . Has . . . Been . . . Chasing . . . My . . . Turkeys . . ." What the book actually says is this: *I am as sure as I stand here, lady, that your dog has been after my turkeys.* The teacher asks Harry to reread the sentence. Harry reads it again, exactly the way he read it before. The teacher tries to make him insert the word "lady" and read "after" instead of "chasing." But Harry is impervious. It is utterly impossible to convince him that *lady* belongs in the sentence or that it makes any difference whatever whether he says "after" or "chasing." Why, he has brought out the meaning of this sentence perfectly, he obviously feels. He doesn't understand what more is wanted of him. It's about your dog chasing my turkeys, isn't it? He reads the sentence a third time, with a proud ring of certainty: "I . . . Am . . . As . . . Sure . . . As . . . I . . . Stand . . . Here . . . That . . . Your . . . Dog . . . Has . . . Been . . . Chasing . . . My . . . Turkeys . . ."

The teacher gives up and calls on little Susan to go on. After all, it's a rainy Monday morning and she has been doing this thing for thirty years. Harry is a poor reader, and she is doing her best. If Harry can't read, it's not her fault. Next year, in fourth grade, Harry will doubtless be classified as a remedial reading case. Perhaps the remedial reading teacher will be able to do something with him. She can give more time to him. There are twenty-four other children in this third grade; there is only one Gerald, but there are several Harrys.

Let's thank the teacher and take our leave. Shall we go into another classroom? Or shall we return tomorrow, or Wednesday, or Thursday? Let me assure you that it won't be necessary. We have seen all there is to be seen. This is it; this is what happens day after day. The three groups, and "Let's start at the top of page 53," and the chant. Ever so often the chant contains words that are not on the page, and then comes the vacant stare and the attempt to remember the right word. As to the "stories," they hardly come into the business at all. Even if the children were able to pick an unfamiliar story in the book, read it once from beginning to end, and understand what it says, they still wouldn't be interested. But they don't read anyway. They perform a daily ritual of chanting certain words while their eyes are fixed on certain marks on paper.

This is the practice that corresponds to the theory of the word method. What I have shown you is *not* exceptional; it is *not* an example of misapplying or misunderstanding the word-method theory. It's the logical outcome of the premises given; you proceed on certain assumptions and you get children who read *at* instead of *it, one two three* instead of *one morning Alice,* and *chasing* instead of *after.* The educators know all about it. It's all described in detail in their books.

"It was found," writes Dr. Arthur I. Gates complacently, "that beginning pupils observed primarily the length of words and depended upon the observation of the length for later recognition when they were given such a series of words as *cow, postman, dress, duck, football,* and *dandelion.* To these children differences in length were the most obvious differentiating factors. When, however, the words presented at the same time were substantially the same in length, the pupils tended to study the words until they found some small but outstanding detail, such as the dot over the *i* in *pig,* the 'funny cross' in *box,* the similar beginning and ending in *window,* and the 'monkey's tail' on the *y* in monkey."

"Sometimes," writes Dr. Donald D. Durrell equally complacently, "the child pays no attention to the word, but notices some other condition which serves as a cue. For example, a child who had successfully read the word *children* on a flash card was unable to read it in a book. He insisted he had never seen the word before. He was presented with a flash card of

the word and was asked how he recognized the word as *children*.
He replied, 'By the smudge over in the corner.' "

"The child's eyes," writes Dr. Edward W. Dolch equally
complacently, "just wandered over the page and back and forth
and up and down. The reason for this habit is most obvious.
For years and years the child has got more from the pictures
than from the text, so he has learned to look constantly up at
the picture during the process of what he calls reading. Look
at a few words and then up at the picture, back at the same
words or different words and then up at the picture. And so on.
Then, if there is no picture, he looks along the lines from some
words he knows to other words he knows and skips on to others
and then back to the previous ones, trying to make sense out
of it all. He has the eye movements of doing a jigsaw puzzle
rather than of reading. This habit of 'jumping eyes' is a tremendous one to unteach."

"A primary grade child," write Dr. Irving H. Anderson
and Dr. Walter F. Dearborn equally complacently, "was given
the following to read:

> This is a cow.
> The cow gives milk.
> Milk is good for boys and girls.

These sentences were constructed from words which appeared
in the basal reader materials used in the school. This, however, is the way in which the child proceeded to read the
sentences:

> This is the way we wash our clothes,
> Wash our clothes,
> Wash our clothes."

After giving several examples of such results of the word
method, Anderson and Dearborn add calmly: "There is no
need to be disillusioned by any of this."

That's what the word method is like in actual practice.

However, this chapter would be incomplete if I gave the impression that the children are never given anything else to read but the so-called stories in the sets of diluted little readers. They are exposed to something else too, at least in some schools. They read "experience charts."

Experience charts were invented by the word-method educators after it had become painfully clear that the material in the readers bored children to death. Somehow the famous "zeal and zest" wasn't forthcoming. What was to be done? The educational pioneers came up with a beautiful answer: Let's give the children some reading matter that deals with their own personal experience.

For an example, here is an "experience chart," as published in *The Teaching of Reading in the Elementary School* by Professor Paul McKee:

OUR TRIP TO THE CREAMERY

We went to the creamery last Monday.
We rode on a big bus.
Miss Clark and Mr. Stone went with us.
We saw butter being made.
We saw cream being separated from milk.
Each of us drank a glass of milk.
We thanked Mr. Brown for helping us.
Then we came home on the bus.

What have we here? We have a little "story" composed by the children themselves, since each of the sentences was offered by one of the children and then put on the blackboard by the teacher. Whether it is more interesting for the children to read about yesterday's trip to the creamery than about Jerry moving to the farm is doubtful. Anyway, they "read" these experience charts in exactly the same fashion as they "read" their readers. "We . . . Went . . . To . . . The . . . Creamery . . . Last . . . Monday . . . We . . ." Where is the advantage in that? The minority among educators who champion the experience approach claim all sorts of miracles. The truth is that it's just as ineffective as the "story" method, with the added feature that there is *no* vocabulary control and *no* planned repetition of words.

Nevertheless, experience charts are the latest gospel. In a recent book by Stuart Chase, *The Power of Words,* the technique is described with great enthusiasm:

When I went to primary school in Boston, the teacher would dictate a sentence and we would try to write it correctly, each at his little desk screwed to the floor, with inkpot in the corner. Today in a New York school, the pupils dictate, and the teacher does the writing—on the blackboard.

"You tell me the story," she says, "and I will put it down. What do you think is the first thing to tell?"

"That we took a trip," says one child.

"Let's start this way," says another. " 'We took a trip to the park to see if we could find any community helpers.' "

"Good," says the teacher and writes it on the board. "Now, think of the next sentence."

" 'We saw the park man,' " suggests a little girl. " 'We asked him for information.' "

Teacher writes again, but takes time out while the children discuss what "information" means. When they have finished the story of about ten sentences, they all read it aloud, feeling some of the pride of authorship, and then copy it into their own books. I am sure this is a big improvement on my school.

Observe the processes involved: first, the children are making a record of an experience they enjoyed; telling a simple story that happened to them, very much as they would tell it to the family at home. They are shown how the spoken story can be arranged in sentences, and how it looks when written down. They go over each sentence at least three times. This is not a lesson in "reading" or "writing" or "spelling" or "discussion," though all are included. *It is the total communication process.*

I think Mr. Chase's enthusiasm for experience charts is misplaced, to say the least. (A footnote tells that the facts are reported in *The New York Times* of April 7, 1953.) Observe, in the first place, that these New York children have been brought to the point that they voluntarily use such jargon as "community helpers." Observe, second, that this is *not* a lesson in reading, since the children only repeat sentences they themselves dictated to the teacher a minute or two before. Observe, third, that this is *not* a lesson in writing, since the children simply copy in their notebooks what they see on the blackboard. Observe, fourth, that this is *not* a lesson in spelling, since the children *dictate* to the teacher and are carefully shielded from the active experience of recording their own words on paper. If this is preparation for life, it is at best preparation for the life of an executive, complete with dictating machine and private secretary.

It may be true, as Mr. Chase points out, that this is a lesson in "discussion." But then, parents do not pay school taxes to have first-graders taught "discussion." They pay to have their children taught to read, write, and spell.

Chapter IX

EYEWITNESS REPORT

This chapter consists of my eyewitness report on the teaching of reading with phonics.

In the course of my research for this book I came across the book *Reading with Phonics* by Julie Hay and Charles E. Wingo, which I mentioned earlier. I learned that one of the authors of that book, the late Miss Hay, had been a teacher in the public schools of the Argo-Summit-Bedford Park school district near Chicago; the other author, Mr. Wingo, was and is superintendent of schools in that district. All the schools in that district teach reading with phonics.

I also learned that the phonetic method developed by the late Professor Leonard Bloomfield was and is used experimentally in some Roman Catholic parochial schools in Chicago.

In March, 1954, after having made the necessary arrangements with Mr. Wingo and with Father Stanley C. Stoga, Assistant Superintendent of Catholic Schools in the Chicago Archdiocese, I went to Chicago to see for myself.

I spent Thursday, March 25, 1954, visiting the schools in the Argo-Summit-Bedford Park district.

The three communities are about ten or fifteen miles outside of Chicago. There is a large plant of the Corn Products Refining Company in Argo; it is a purely industrial suburb, as are Summit and Bedford Park. The people who live there are working-class people; there is a sizable colored population, and one of the schools in the district is all colored. On that Thursday last March the whole neighborhood looked poor, bleak, shabby—the last place in the world where you would expect to find a great experiment in education.

I first went into a first-grade classroom in the W. W. Walker School in Bedford Park. There were twenty-three children in that class. The teacher's name was Miss Mary Hletko.

Miss Hletko explained to me that it was the usual practice to work through the Hay-Wingo primer during the first year and to review it in the second and then again in the third year. This year, however, with this particular class, she had finished the book in the first semester.

She had divided the children in the usual manner into three groups. There were twelve in the top group, six in the middle group, and five in the poorest group.

The children made an excellent impression on me. They were alert, polite, and well behaved. During the hour that I spent with them, Miss Hletko had no occasion to use any discipline. They were not at all fazed by having a visitor present in the classroom. They were clearly interested in what they were doing and obviously enjoying themselves.

Miss Hletko first had them write sentences on the blackboard about things that had happened the day before. This was something on the order of the experience charts I described in the last chapter. But the difference was tremendous. These first-graders didn't dictate to their teacher. They wrote their experience charts themselves!

This is what they wrote on the blackboard, each of five children doing one sentence, while I was looking on:

Last night it rained with thunder and lightning.
Our footbridge was washed away.
I saw a lot of dead worms on our front porch.
The worms crawled out of the ground to keep from drowning.
The ditches overflowed and the water ran off into all the yards.

I am not pretending that the children performed this task quickly and flawlessly. It took quite some time to get all those words on the blackboard, and in maybe half a dozen places Miss Hletko had to help them with their spelling—not spelling the words for them, to be sure, but reminding them of phonetic rules they had learned. In each case they finally did remember the rule and spelled the word correctly.

Naturally, considering the fact that there had been a great storm and a flood in the Chicago area the day before, there was a lot of excited talk about the subject matter of those sentences, and the children went through this activity in anything but a mechanical fashion.

Next, Miss Hletko, for my benefit, picked up a copy of that morning's Chicago *Tribune* and let the children read sentences from the paper. However, I wanted to make 100 per cent sure of my facts. With her permission I took the newspaper myself and began to call children at random. Here are some of the paragraphs they read for me:

Police Commissioner O'Connor said yesterday that policemen will begin a house to house canvass tomorrow to assure that Chicago dog owners comply with the rabies quarantine imposed last December.

Suburban Riverside's policemen were ordered yesterday to capture, dead or alive, a brown squirrel named Marge. The hunt means a great deal to the 10 year old girl who was bitten by the creature on Tuesday.

The weather man is going to get up earlier than the farmer this summer to give the farmer an up-to-the-minute report on the day's weather outlook with his breakfast.

The first midwest postage stamp show, sponsored by the Chicago chapter of the American Stamp Dealers' Association, will be held tomorrow thru Sunday in the La Salle hotel. More than 10,000 are expected to attend. A part of the stamp collection of ex-King Farouk of Egypt will be exhibited.

Of course these first-graders didn't read the newspaper items in the way an adult would. They had a good deal of difficulty. Miss Hletko had to tell them what the symbol 10,000 stood for. She had to help them over some of the harder words, and in one instance—*Egypt*—the child was unable to work out the right pronunciation.

But the fact is, and I testify to it, that those children read what was in the paper. They were perfectly able to pronounce words they had never seen before, according to reasonable phonetic principles. The child, for instance, who read the item about ex-King Farouk, pronounced the *ou* in *Farouk* as in *house*. Another child, who read a headline REPORTS PROGRESS IN TREATMENT OF ATOMIC SICKNESS, pronounced the word *atomic* correctly, but put the accent on the first syllable. Needless to say, that six-year-old child hadn't the slightest idea of what the word meant. How could he? My point is that after six months in school he could read the word off the page.

Another boy read, and pronounced correctly, the word *canvass* in the first of the paragraphs I quoted. Just as a check, I asked him whether he knew the meaning of the word. He thought for a while, then said he had heard about canvas shoes. Which means that he *didn't* know the word in the sense that it was used in the newspaper item. What he did know, however, was that the combination of letters, *c, a, n, v, a, s, s* stands for the sequence of sounds that makes up the word *canvass*.

After this interlude, Miss Hletko reverted to her normal procedure. There followed a period of reading. I learned that the poorest group was at that time reading the Scott, Foresman reader designed for the first half of second grade; the middle group was halfway through the Scott, Foresman reader for the first half of third grade; and the best group—consisting of twelve of the twenty-three children—was reading the Scott, Foresman reader for the *second* half of third grade.

The children in the best group started to read. I picked up

the book—which was clearly marked "32" on the back—and asked them to read a story way back which they had never seen before. They started to read.

What happened then impressed me even more than the astonishing performances on the blackboard and with the Chicago *Tribune*. These children did *not* go through the ritual that I had seen performed dozens of times in another school. They did *not* chant the words, one by one, laboriously and insecurely, in a monotonous, one-word-after-another singsong. Instead, they did something that I had seen done in no other classroom. *They read the story!* They went through the pages, at a pretty fast clip, with completely natural intonation, laughing spontaneously at one place, expressing surprise at another, following the thread of the story with animated suspense.

Afterward they talked a little about the characters and incidents of the story. (It was something about a pioneer family and a bear.) As a matter of fact, I myself had paid more attention to the performance of the children than to the contents of the story. I realized with a delighted shock that they remembered considerably more of the story than I did.

Finally I left Miss Hletko's first grade and visited some other classrooms in the same building. I found that another first grade had not yet finished the Hay-Wingo primer and was reading a second-grade reader. I found that in second grade they were reviewing the primer and were reading a third-grade book. I then spent some time in a sixth grade.

The sixth-graders were the products of a school system that starts with first-graders like those in Miss Hletko's class. They were bright, lively, and well behaved. Their teacher showed me a chart with the results of a recent achievement test *in all subjects*. There was quite a spread of the grade levels attained by the twenty-one students in the class. In the right-hand lower corner of the chart, however, was a single figure, showing the average grade level achievement of the whole class in all subjects. That figure was 7.5. These sixth-graders, by March, had reached the standard seventh-graders in other schools reach about January or February. (Note that this confirms precisely my rule-of-thumb that phonics teaching saves one year, not only in reading but in all subjects. If the children in Bedford Park had started first grade at five, they would now be *two years* ahead of what is generally accepted as the norm in American schools—or on a par with children in England or on the Continent of Europe.)

The sixth-graders showed me some of the compositions they had written. They read a few of those papers aloud. The compositions were competent, intelligently written and, as far as I could see, practically free of spelling errors.

The class had copies of *My Weekly Reader,* which dealt that week with Pakistan. We got into quite a discussion on the subject, and then somehow got onto the topic of communism. The children talked about it with understanding and a good deal of sense.

Then, to finish the demonstration, they read—fluently— from junior high school textbooks in science and social studies.

I took my leave. In the afternoon I spent an hour or two in the Argo school—the school that serves the colored section. The picture was much the same. To be sure, many of those children came from homes without reading matter; some of the parents were probably illiterate. Obviously the children's average I.Q. was lower than that of the children of Bedford Park. But the difference between the Argo school and a typical word-method school was still striking. I visited a first grade and a second grade. In the second grade the children did a pretty good job of writing on the blackboard. Then they read from a second-grade reader. They read fluently, with natural intonation, and with much understanding and enjoyment. In other words, *they read the story.*

Later that afternoon I talked with Mr. Wingo in his office. He told me that his primer was used, of course, in all four elementary schools in the district. The results were always the same: general student achievement about one grade level above the national norm in all subjects; no "non-readers" except for children that were clearly feeble-minded. The situation had also carried over into the high school. The high-school students performed beautifully; an extraordinary number of them qualified for scholarships at good colleges and universities; all of them gobbled up a fabulous number of books. The amount Mr. Wingo—with the happy approval of his school board—spends for library books is five or more times what is spent by the ordinary school system: $5 to $8 per child annually.

The parents of Argo, Summit, and Bedford Park are naturally proud that their children are doing so well. They know that Bedford Park first-graders have exhibited their reading skill to goggle-eyed teachers and parents at Oak Park and other wealthy Chicago suburbs; they also know that nationally known educators like Dr. William S. Gray of the University of Chicago and Dr. Paul A. Witty of Northwestern University have visited their classrooms. Mr. Wingo, unlike practically all other school superintendents in the country, is not on the defensive.

He also told me something about Miss Hay, the original author of the method embodied in the primer. Miss Hay never had any other title or office than that of grade-school teacher in Argo. For twenty years she developed the system on the basis of her daily classroom experience—and her deep, intuitive understanding of the way children's minds work. She herself had been brought up on the Beacon method; but she felt she could improve upon that method—and did.

When Mr. Wingo came to Argo as the new superintendent, he had a son, then in fourth grade, who couldn't read. Miss Hay undertook to teach the boy, giving him half-hour private lessons every morning before school. Young Mr. Wingo, a recent college graduate, has not forgotten Miss Hay; neither has his father. Neither, apparently, has anyone else who ever met her—a woman completely devoted to her life's chosen task.

I returned from Argo to Chicago and next morning, with Father Stoga, visited St. Roman school.

St. Roman is one of eight Chicago parochial schools run by the community of the Sisters of St. Joseph. (In all of these eight schools the experiment with the Bloomfield system is in operation.) St. Roman is way over on the south side of Chicago; the children's parents are working-class people, mostly of Polish extraction.

I visited a first grade, a second grade, a third grade and a sixth grade. The difference between what I saw there and what I had seen the day before at Argo was striking. The atmosphere was considerably more formal; there was a good deal of old-fashioned, unashamed drill; the pace seemed ten times slower. In the first grade the children, one by one, went through exercises embodying the loud spelling-out of words; in the second grade they did long, patient drill work on suffixes —the kind of work that most public-school children do in fourth grade, if at all.

In the third grade Father Stoga asked to have some fourth-grade science and social studies texts brought in, and called on the children at random to read aloud. They read fluently and with full understanding. When they came across a word they hadn't seen before, they instantly and automatically read it according to phonetic rules. One such word, I remember, was the word *athletics*. It took that third-grade boy a little while to pronounce it right; but as soon as he did so, he knew what he had read.

In the sixth grade Father Stoga asked the students about their extracurricular reading. Most of them immediately produced some book they had in their desk—all sorts of books, of good caliber. At least one of the boys was reading an adult book— a fat novel dealing with the life of fishermen.

Again we had seventh- and eighth-grade textbooks brought in, which the students opened at random and read for us. One was a science text and the girl who read it stumbled over the word *molecular,* which of course she had never seen before. She accented it, with perfect phonetic sense, on the first syllable. Later she came across the word *capillaries.* Without hesitation she read that unknown word off the page, pronouncing it "*capill*aries." Millions of sixth-graders across the country would be utterly unable to read that word.

After we had seen the sixth grade, Father Stoga and I went to lunch. He filled me in on some details—the kind of details I was expecting by now. It is "normal" for pupils in St. Roman school (and the other schools where the Bloomfield method is used) to be one year ahead of the national norm in all subjects. In fact, Father Stoga gave me copies of two unpublished papers of his, filled to the brim with statistics showing that one-year differential.

There are no "non-readers" at St. Roman. If a child is slow in catching on to reading, his teacher pays a little special attention to his work in phonics, and that's that.

The materials used in those schools are those originally developed by Dr. Bloomfield, printed and adapted for classroom use by the Sisters of St. Joseph. (I studied the materials later and found them practically identical with Bloomfield's own, unpublished manuscript.)

Father Stoga told me that the experiment has so far been fully successful and is to be carried on indefinitely. Years ago, he said, a good many prominent educators came to see the method in operation; and for the second time in two days, I heard mention of the names of Dr. William S. Gray and Dr. Paul A. Witty. But lately, Father Stoga added, the interest seems to have died down.

And here ends my eyewitness report. What does it prove? I think it proves conclusively three things:

1. If you teach reading with phonics (regardless of the particular method used), student achievement in all subjects will be, on the average, one grade higher than the national norm.

2. If you teach reading with phonics, you will have no cases of "non-readers."

3. If you teach reading with phonics, you will produce students with a habit of wide reading.

You may say at this point—if you are a die-hard defender of the word method—that my evidence is still not conclusive. You may ask for *more* data, *more* experiments, *more* statistics. You may want other rigidly controlled tests to check on the facts that I reported here, and still more tests to check on the results of those tests.

There is no answer to this sort of argument. Conclusive evidence, in the end, means evidence that makes you feel satisfied you have found the truth. Perhaps you are the kind of person who will never be satisfied, even if I presented ten thousand cases of phonics-trained mental giants and ten thousand word-method trained "non-readers" who are their identical twins.

As for me, I know that nothing could be more conclusive than those twelve nice, normal American children in Miss Hletko's class who had such fun reading the bear story in the third-grade book—in March of their first year in school. Either that was a miracle or every word in this book is true.

Chapter X

WORD GUESSING—ITS CAUSE AND CURE

Although you may not think so, my main purpose in writing this book is not to criticize and attack the doctrines of the educators. What I am really interested in is a book that will be of practical help to parents.

You are a mother or a father. Your child—or your children—have trouble with reading. What can you do about it?

Let me spell out in so many words what I am trying to say in this book. Your child's trouble with reading comes solely from the fact that in school he has been taught word guessing instead of reading—and by reading I mean getting the meaning of words formed by letters on a printed page, and nothing else. As long as he cannot say out loud what each letter combination stands for, he cannot read. Memorizing or guessing the meaning of whole words is *not* reading; on the contrary, it is an acquired bad habit that stands in the way of your child's ever learning to read properly. Therefore, the problem of improving your child's reading cannot be solved by giving him a more concentrated dose of what he has been getting since first grade. It can only be solved by making him *drop* the habit of word guessing and teaching him to read—from scratch.

Of course, an ounce of prevention is better than a pound of cure. By far the best thing you can do is to teach your child to read before he ever *gets* into the habit of word guessing. My advice is, teach your child yourself how to read—at the age of five.

This is wholly in the American tradition. It's what the

pioneers did, when there were no schools for hundreds of miles around. You, of course, are in a different position: there is a public school within easy reach, supported by your own taxes. However, the fact is—let's face it—that this school is not doing the job you want to have done; neither does any other public or private school you can send your child to. You want your child to be taught reading; instead, the schools teach word guessing. So, why not do the job yourself? You paint your living room, you lay tiles in your kitchen, you do dozens of things that used to be left to professional experts. Why not take on instruction in reading? Surely you can do a simple job like that. Millions of English and American parents have done it before you; all it amounts to is teaching your child the meanings of twenty-six letters and some fifty letter combinations, in small letters and capitals. If you start in the fall of the year when your child is five, you have a whole year to do the job before the school can do any damage to your child's mental habits. What's stopping you? Do it yourself—and the problem will be solved once and for all.

You say your child isn't ready at the age of five? Don't be ridiculous. Are you trying to tell me that your child is inferior to every single child born and brought up in Great Britain?

You say you haven't got the time? I don't believe it. Of course you have the time. You have the time to play with your child, haven't you? Play a little reading with him. Reading at the age of five is nothing but a game.

You say you are not up to the job? Yes, you are. Let me show you how it's done.

You start with the letters and what they stand for. Go very slow. Take weeks or even months for that first step. Make quite sure your child *knows* that *A* means the first sound in *apple, M* means *mmmmmmmm,* and *S* means *sssssss.*

When he does know, and can also write each of the letters he has learned, start with three-letter words, containing the short vowels. Go on from there, in the sequence shown in this book.

Be patient: always wait until your child has fully mastered the last lesson before you go on to the next. Always combine reading and writing; if it takes more time to do it that way, take more time. You have a whole year; a whole year is an enormously long time in the life of a five-year-old.

You don't have to wait a whole year, though, before you can give your child stories to read. Let him learn how it feels to read; if you teach him phonics right along, he won't be confused by "unphonetic" words like *was* and *done*.

What stories should be read at this stage? Obviously *not* the Dick-and-Jane or Alice-and-Jerry type of thing. Rather, give him the classic stories that have always been enjoyed by small children—nursery tales, simple fairy tales, animal fables. Give him *The Old Woman and Her Pig, The Cat and the Mouse, Henny Penny, The Gingerbread Boy, The House That Jack Built, The Three Little Pigs, The Half-Chick,* and *The Three Billy Goats Gruff.* Give him Aesop's *The Fox and the Stork, The Milk Maid, The Wind and the Sun, The Lion and the Mouse, The Fox and the Grapes, Belling the Cat,* and *Country Mouse and City Mouse.* Pretty soon the story reading will reenforce the phonics lessons and the phonics drills will help him read the stories. Before long, and before you really know it, he will take over and teach himself the rest of the letters and words.

Probably the process will *not* take a whole year. Remember that so far in this book I have talked about classroom teaching. Now I am talking about private, individual tutoring at home—the most speedy and efficient method of teaching there is. Chances are that by spring your child will be a pretty good reader—like the children in Miss Hletko's class in Bedford Park.

Then you'll be faced by a problem hardly any American parent has any more: the problem of how to quench your child's thirst for books. But it's not really a difficult problem: just give him the books parents usually read aloud to children of his age. And later, as he grows up, give him the books children of his age have always liked: fairy tales, mythology, adventure stories, Stevenson, Mark Twain, Poe . . . he'll be all right. Just turn him loose in a public library, and let him take over his own education.

But let's go back to his—or her—kindergarten days. What primer should you use? Well, naturally I tried to write this book so that in a pinch it could be used for that purpose. But I am not recommending that to you. The best available book for the purpose is the one I mentioned several times before: *Reading With Phonics* by Julie Hay and Charles E. Wingo. You can get it for $2.40 from J. B. Lippincott Company, 333 West Lake Street, Chicago 6, Illinois. There is also a Teachers' Edition at $4.00, which contains the Pupils' Edition plus 128 pages of suggestions on how to teach the material. The book is well illustrated. To my knowledge, it is the only available American phonetic primer. (You can also get the Beacon materials from Ginn & Company in England, 7 Queen Square, London, WC 1, but there is a whole stack of materials and classroom devices instead of a single book, and anyway you probably won't want to get your books all the way from England.)

When your home-taught child enters school at the age of six, he'll know how to read. He'll be bored stiff during all those hours spent on the diluted little readers, but there is nothing that can be done about that. What's more important, he'll be immune to the word-guessing habit from there on. He'll be safe. As far as he is concerned—and you—reading has ceased to be a problem.

If, at the time you are reading this, your child is in first, second, or third grade, proceed according to the same plan, with suitable adaptations. Get the Hay-Wingo book—or use this book—and give your child home lessons in phonics, fortifying him as much as possible against the word guessing he is exposed to in school.

Beginning with fourth grade, however, your procedure should be somewhat different. By that time your child will doubtless have become a confirmed, inveterate word guesser.

Presumably, since you are reading this book, you have a child who is a remedial reading case. In a sense that's too bad, since the problem is exactly the same whether your child is a "non-reader" or a perfect reader according to current educational standards. I wish the parents of good readers would also read this book *and apply it.* They would discover what their children could really do—every single one of them could do school work at least one year ahead of the national norm if he knew how to read properly.

However, let's see what you can do to help your Johnny who is in fourth, fifth, or sixth grade and can't read. (And at this point I should explain why I keep talking about "Johnny." It's an established fact that 80 per cent of all the "non-readers" are boys. The educators have dozens of theories about this mysterious sex differential; girls, they tell us, are more intelligent, more visual, more verbal, more whatnot. The simple truth is, I think, that girls are usually a little less revolted by the stupidity of the word method than boys. Teach children phonics, and there won't be any sex differential in their achievement, as there is none in England, in Germany, in France, and in the rest of the world.)

To begin with, let's try to isolate Johnny from his word-guessing environment. While he is in school, that is difficult or almost impossible. So the best thing will be to work with him during summer vacations. Let him stop all reading—all *attempts* to read. Explain to him that now he is going to learn how to read, and that for the time being, books are out. All he'll get for several months are lessons in phonics.

This, incidentally, is important. Take him fully into your confidence and explain to him exactly what you are trying to do. Tell him that you are going to do something new with him—something entirely different from what his teachers did in school. Tell him that this is *certain* to work. Convince him that as soon as he has taken this medicine he will be cured.

Then start him on the phonics exercises. At this age the Hay-Wingo book would probably arouse his antagonism. So give him either this book or the only other book of that type that I know: *Remedial Reading Drills* by Thorleif G. Hegge, Samuel A. Kirk, and Winifred D. Kirk. (George Wahr Publishing Company, Ann Arbor, Michigan, $1.50.) Go with him through the drills, one by one, always making sure that he has mastered the previous one before you go on to the next.

Only when you are through—or almost through—with the drills and exercises, start him again on reading. At first, let him read aloud to you. Watch like a hawk that he doesn't guess a single word. Interrupt him every time he does it and let him work out the word phonetically. He'll never learn to read if he doesn't get over the word-guessing habit.

There is a real problem in what to give him to read at this time. It must be something that will interest him, something that he can get through within a reasonable time, and yet something that won't frustrate him. If you give him fairy tales, he'll be bored; if you give him regular books written for a boy his age, he'll bog down.

At the risk of being called inconsistent, I recommend to you *The American Adventure Series,* edited by Dr. Emmett A. Betts of Temple University, Philadelphia, and published by the Wheeler Publishing Company, 2831-35 South Parkway, Chicago 16, Illinois. This is a series of brief books, specially written and edited for poor readers in fourth, fifth, and sixth grade. Naturally, these books are based on the word-method theory, which means that they have a rigidly controlled vocabulary. However, at least they face up to the problem. Their prime purpose is to interest boys. If you start Johnny on one, two, or three of these books, he will learn what it means to read a book.

After that, you may switch to exciting adventure stories and poetry. With my own pupil "Johnny," I used, among other things, the famous short story "The Most Dangerous Game" by Richard Connell. It was highly successful. I also let him read the poem "Invictus" by William Ernest Henley.

> Out of the night that covers me,
> Black as the pit from pole to pole,
> I thank whatever gods may be
> For my unconquerable soul. . . .

I'll never forget the thrill I felt when Johnny read the word *unconquerable* off the page.

The reading "experts" of course will say that such a program of remedial reading is much too simple. What about Johnny's emotional troubles, what about such nervous habits as reversals, what about correcting his eye movements? But my answer to all of that is phonics. Phonics is the key.

As to emotional problems, *of course,* Johnny has emotional problems. So has every child—see Gesell and Ilg's monumental work. To be sure, in Johnny's case those problems are aggravated. They are aggravated because the poor child for years has been treated as an outcast, because everybody has told him incessantly that he is too stupid to learn the most essential thing there is to learn, because he has been scolded, ridiculed, badgered, punished, and made to feel miserable ever since he first came into contact with books. Naturally he has emotional problems. Teach him phonics, and most of them will disappear like snow in the sun.

He also may be one of the famous reversal cases—he may read *saw* for *was, nip* for *pin,* and so on. What's so mysterious about that? He has been taught for years that words must be read as wholes, that the general shape of a word is the only thing that counts. So, if he is left-handed, or otherwise inclined to tackle things differently from other people, he'll occasionally grasp one of those whole-word shapes from right to left instead of from left to right. What difference does it make? Nobody has ever told him that it *does* make a difference. If he had been taught phonics from the start, if he had never known anything else than reading words letter by letter from left to right, he would never have made a single reversal mistake in his life.

And his eye movements? His eye movements correspond to the reading method he has been taught. Teach him phonics, and his eyes will accommodate themselves to his improved mental habits.

Remedial reading nowadays relies largely on retraining the eyes. The work done by the eyes is poor, so the theory goes, let's teach the eyes to do a better job. Hence all the mechanical gadgets, the films, the tachistoscopes, the reading accelerators, and so forth.

Actually, the relationship of eye movements to reading is very simple. The eyes wander along a line across the page, stopping from time to time to pick up a word or two or three, then moving on to the next stop, and the next, and the next. Sometimes the eyes jump back, to correct a mistake in reading. So, technically speaking, there are only three important mechanical elements in the reading process: the average duration of fixation pauses, the width of the average fixation span, and the average number of regression movements.

Now, it is clear that *any* improvement in reading will and must reduce the number of regression movements. The better you read, the less often you will have to go back to correct an error.

The basic problem of remedial reading therefore boils down to this: The eyes of the slow, poor reader stop for too long and take in too little. To improve his reading, he must either shorten his fixation pauses or widen his fixation span.

Every single one of the current reading improvement gadgets and techniques is designed to widen the student's fixation span. The word-method theory says you must read whole words; to improve your reading, you must therefore learn to grab larger gobs of words off the page. In other words, the gadgets force you to do the same kind of word guessing you have done before, but do it faster and more of it. You may improve your reading speed this way, but your reading will doubtless be less accurate than it was.

If, however, you improve your reading by learning phonics, your fixation span will probably stay the same, but your fixation *pauses* will get shorter; you'll gradually learn to *see* the letters on the page more quickly. This fact is known from studies of the way musicians read music; they learn to read music note by note—which corresponds to learning to read words letter by letter—and the better they read the faster their eyes move from one fixation point to the next. Their fixation span, however, stays much the same. (If you're interested, you'll find more details on this in "The Study of Eye Movements in Reading" by Professor Miles A. Tinker, *Psychological Bulletin,* March, 1946.)

All of which means that remedial reading courses concentrate on exactly the opposite of what they should: they strengthen the bad habit of word guessing instead of trying to cure it.

And here let me add a word in case you are interested in improving your own reading. Obviously I am saying that the currently fashionable speed-reading courses and programs won't do you much good. What then *should* you do?

I hesitate to mention it, but what you should do is something you are not likely to do at all, human nature being what it is: you should learn to read all over again from scratch. Ideally, you should take time out from your reading and begin the phonics exercises in this book, or in Hay-Wingo, or in Hegge-Kirk, and do them faithfully from beginning to end.

Let me defend this "impossible" suggestion with a simple analogy. Suppose you are a garden-variety, hunt-and-peck typist —like me, sitting here at the typewriter and making innumerable horrible, ghastly mistakes. You know as well as I do that the only way to improve hunt-and-peck typing is to start all

over again and learn the touch system by dint of pure, unadulterated, old-fashioned drill. Do I do it? No. I don't expect
you to do it either. But you see what I mean, don't you?

Think about it. Are you a word guesser or a real reader?
When you read something about an ancient, do you tend to
read the word as "accident"? When you read something about
some sliver, do you tend to read the word as "silver"? Are you
a surefooted phonetic speller? Here are a few words in phonetic
transcription. Would you know how to spell them?

> *baz*-ight
> alt*rish*-l
> rayzh-n
> *prig*-ess
> perry-*klayzh*a
> unshl

Are you sure you would automatically spell these words *bazzite,
altricial, rasion, priggess, periclasia,* and *uncial?* Or could you
too use a little phonics?

How about doing those exercises *with* Johnny?

Chapter XI

A LETTER TO JOHNNY'S TEACHER

Dear Miss Smith:

I cannot end this book without a chapter directly addressed to you. Of course you realize that I am mainly writing for parents. But I know that a good many teachers will read this book, and there are a few things that I want to talk to you about specially.

We have met several times during the past year. In fact, I talked with you once or twice about this book and what I was trying to do. Your attitude was like that of most teachers, I suppose. You said, in effect, "Phonics is all right, but . . ." And your principal, Mr. Robinson, has said much the same thing to me a number of times. "Oh, but we do give them phonics," he answered whenever I brought up the subject. His conscience was clear. In his school, he explained to me proudly, they use the best features of *all* methods. There is a lot to be said for phonics, and *of course* phonics is used too.

I am sure Mr. Robinson has said the same sort of thing to parents a thousand times. It is, on the surface, an unassailable answer. Mothers come in and complain that their children are not taught phonics. The answer is that this school *does* teach phonics. The mother just didn't know; other schools may be lacking in this respect; but this school, no. What are you complaining about, lady? We do give them phonics.

The trouble with this is that we are not talking about the same thing: the phonics the mothers and I are talking about is not the same phonics that you and Mr. Robinson mean. We

mean phonics as a way to learn reading. We mean phonics that
is taught to the child letter by letter and sound by sound until
he knows it—and when he knows it he knows how to read.
We mean phonics as a complete, systematic subject—the sum
total of information about the phonetic rules by which English
is spelled. We mean phonics as it was taught in this country
until some thirty years ago, and as it is taught all over the
world today. There is no room for misunderstanding, is there?
We say, and we cannot be budged, that when you learn phonics, in our sense of the word, you learn how to read. We want
our children taught this particular set of facts and rules, because we know that this and only this will do the job.

But when you and Mr. Robinson talk about phonics, you
mean something entirely different. You mean phonics as one
among a dozen things that come into the teaching of reading.
You mean that on a Wednesday in May, out of the blue and
with nothing before and after it, you go to the blackboard
and show the children that the word *pin* with an *e* at the end
makes *pine*. The children thereupon dutifully "learn" that fact.
They are not shown that the same principle holds for *a, e,
o,* and *u;* they are not shown that it also applies to *pining* and
tiny; they are not told what short and long vowels there are;
they are not told that *i* also makes the sound of *ir* in bird and
the sound of *ie* in *pie*. No. They are given "incidental," "intrinsic" phonics. On a Friday in June they will be told that *tch*
in *catch* stands for the sound of *ch*. Next year in October they
may hear about *nk* as in *pink*.

Let's understand each other. Systematic phonics is one thing,
unsystematic phonics is another. Systematic phonics is *the* way
to teach reading, unsystematic phonics is nothing—an occa-
sional excursion into something that has nothing whatever to do
with the method used to fix words in the child's mind. Either
you tell a child that the word is *trip* because the letter sounds
add up to "trip" and nothing else—or you tell him, "Don't you
remember, we had the word last week, in the story about the

trip to the woods." Phonics is *not* "one of many techniques the child can use to unlock the meaning of words" (you can't possibly imagine how sick I am of all this jargon)—phonics is simply the knowledge of the way spoken English is put on paper.

Among other things, this means that there is an end to phonics. Phonics is something that a child can master completely, once and for all, with the assurance that he has covered everything there is. This is of tremendous emotional significance to the child—and to an adult too, for that matter. Reading, he sees, is something that can be learned from A to Z—or let's rather say, from the sound of *a* in *apple* to the sound of *zh* in *vision*. There are a known number of items to be mastered and when he is through he knows how to read. You are a teacher, Miss Smith. You *must* know what it means to anyone learning a given subject when there is an end to the book, when he knows that at the bottom of page 128 he will be through. So and so many pages covered, so and so many still to go. There is a concrete goal. Talk about motivation—what better motivation could there conceivably be than the knowledge that at the end of page 128 *he will have learned how to read?*

And now think of your word method. Four hundred words this year, four hundred words the next, four hundred words the year after that. How many words are there in the English language? The child doesn't know. What he does know is that there is an ocean of them. He feels—correctly—that this way he'll never get through. No job in the world could be more heartbreakingly hopeless than learning to read word by word. Will it ever end? The child knows perfectly well that it won't. He'll go through life forever trying to learn more words. He doesn't *want* to learn more words; there are other things in life he's more interested in; he hates the whole business; he wants nothing more than to break out of this never-ending daily routine; and so at one point or other he gives up. If he does it early—in first or second grade—he becomes a "non-reader" (it's your jargon, not mine); if he does it later on, he becomes just an ordinary typical American. The other day I talked to a young insurance executive whom I met in the street. I happened to carry a rather fat book in my hand. He glanced at it and said, by way of conversation, "It's wonderful how you can read these things. Would take me a year to get through."

Of course I can understand your attitude toward phonics. Ever since you went to teachers' college, you have been exposed to derogatory comments on it. Not once in your life have you heard a good word said about it—by your colleagues, that is, by professional educators. Of course parents always holler about it, but that's just because they don't know any better, isn't it? As far as your profession goes, phonics is out of date, unscientific, inefficient, hopelessly defeated and disproven. Oh yes, the books mention it—and I suppose the courses in education too, occasionally—but what is mentioned is always your kind of phonics and not mine. "One among many techniques . . . another method of word attack . . ."—you know what I mean. What it all amounts to is insult added to injury. They have thrown phonics out the window, and now they act as if the evil deed had never happened.

I know how you feel after reading this book. Here is one little book by another one of those cranks, and on the other side is the whole literature on reading—Gates, Gray, Witty, Durrell, and every single one of the other "authorities." Why should you take me seriously?

I'll tell you why. Because all those professors are experts in reading, supposedly, but not experts in either of the two sciences that really deal with reading. Reading isn't a subject that can be studied all by itself. It's a mental activity connected with one aspect of the English language. There are only two kinds of experts worth listening to when it comes to reading: linguists and psychologists.

As to the linguists, they are unanimous on this matter. They are all on my side. I have cited the dean of American linguists, the late Professor Bloomfield of Yale University, repeatedly in this book. Just for the fun of it, let me quote one more linguist, Dr. Robert A. Hall, Jr., Associate Professor of Linguistics at Cornell: "Years of each child's school life could be saved that are now wasted in an inefficient way of learning to read and spell."

With the psychologists it is different. (By psychologists I don't mean educators and teachers' college professors who happen to be members of the American Psychological Association. I mean scholars whose main work is the study of the human mind.) There are, as you know, all kinds of schools. Psychologists are not unanimous on reading because they are not unanimous on anything.

The educators usually say—I have seen that statement dozens of times—that the word method of teaching reading is based on Gestalt psychology. Actually, that statement is completely wrong. The word method is one of the purest applications of conditioned reflex psychology that have ever been invented.

Let me go into this a little further. The Gestalt psychologists say that we don't learn things piecemeal, but by suddenly understanding the total structure of a thing. A face, for instance, or a melody—we see it or hear it as a whole, not feature by feature or note by note. Learning, to a Gestalt psychologist, is not a matter of memorizing the different elements of the thing to be learned, but of grasping the whole thing at once.

The reading "experts" always say that this is what they mean. Let's not teach the child one letter after another, let's teach him whole words. That's Gestalt psychology, they say; teach the whole before the parts.

Actually, if you asked a true Gestalt psychologist to work out a system for teaching reading, he would emerge from his laboratory with phonics. You see, in this system of psychology the only thing that counts is structure, how a thing is put together, the unique way the parts make up the whole. So, if

you want to teach a child how to read the word *chicken,* using
a Gestalt psychology approach, you would try to make him
"see" at a glance that the *c* and the *h* belong together, making
up the *ch,* that the *ck* also is a close letter combination, that the
i before the *ck* necessarily must be a short vowel, and that
the *en* is just an unaccented ending. You would definitely *not*
try to make the child swallow the word *chicken* as a whole—
in a lump, so to speak—without making him understand the
way it is built.

The key to Gestalt psychology is the sudden moment of insight, the flash, the click, the psychological experience of having
everything fall into place. A phonics-trained child learns
chicken that way, and *elephant,* and *hippopotamus,* and *inter-
nationalism,* and every other word in the English language.
He comes across the word for the first time, he recalls to his
mind his knowledge of letters and sounds, and something clicks
in his mind. Why, *that's* what it means! He has learned to read
another word.

You are a teacher, Miss Smith. You *must* know what I am
talking about. It's what makes teaching such a wonderfully
rewarding job. You try to make the children see and understand, and there comes the moment of insight; their faces light
up, and they have learned. It's the visible sign of the creative
job that makes up your life. Yes, indeed, the Gestalt psychologists got hold of something very deep and very basic to human
experience. Let's not saddle them with the theory that led to
the invention of the word method. They deserve better than
that.

I wish the educators were frank about this thing and
admitted that the word method is a simple application of the
conditioned reflex. It goes straight back to Pavlov and his
famous salivating dogs. You remember what Pavlov did, don't
you? He rang a bell whenever he put meat in front of the dog.
The dog salivated whenever he saw meat. So he got used to
salivating whenever he heard a bell. Whereupon Pavlov played

his dirty trick on the poor animal and rang the bell *without* giving him any meat. And the dog salivated in vain. Pavlov had given him a useless, unnatural, totally meaningless conditioned reflex.

It was not long before the conditioned-reflex psychologists —the "associationist" or "connectionist" school—found out that Pavlov's discovery can be used to train a human being. Expose him repeatedly to an association of certain things or events, and sooner or later he will automatically connect them in his mind. *Of course* you can teach a child to read that way —nothing easier than that. You show him the word *chicken* seventeen times in succession, each time in connection with a picture of a chicken and an explanation by the teacher that this combination of letters means a chicken. And so with every other word.

Don't you see how degrading this whole process is? The child is never told *why* this heap of letters means "chicken," and not "giraffe," or "kangaroo," or "recess period." Don't you know that the main question in all children's minds is the question why? Maybe the child would like to know why *chicken* means a chicken, maybe he doesn't ask the question simply because he feels he won't get an answer. It's "chicken" because Teacher says so. Conditioning is an authoritarian process.

It seems to me a plain fact that the word method consists essentially of treating children as if they were dogs. It is not a method of teaching at all; it is clearly a method of animal training. It's the most inhuman, mean, stupid way of foisting something on a child's mind.

Gestalt psychologists don't treat animals that way. On the contrary, they are famous for experiments where they teach chimpanzees to reach bananas with a stick. Instead of training human beings as if they were animals, they proceed on the opposite assumption that you can teach animals to think as if they were human. Gestalt psychologists are humanists, conditioned-reflexers are authoritarians.

Of course, Gestalt psychology isn't the only thing the educators offer to justify their methods. To hear them talk, the word method is the only method of teaching reading that fits into the whole of modern educational theory. It's all part and parcel, they say, of modern, enlightened education.

I say it isn't so. Throughout this book, as you may have noticed, I have carefully refrained from the kind of attacks on progressive education that are now so fashionable in certain quarters. The fact is, I am on the whole on the side of progressive education. I have a Ph.D. degree from Teachers College, Columbia, and I am a sincere admirer of John Dewey. I think education should be democratic, free of senseless formalism and drill, based on interest and meaningful experience, and inseparably joined to the real life that goes on around the child. I have four published books to testify to the fact that I am not a reactionary but a liberal.

But where does all that come into the question of teaching reading? Who says a progressive, liberal-minded teacher must not tell her pupils anything about sounds and letters, but must do nothing but condition them to the sight of certain words? Why is the word method always labeled modern and phonics always branded as reactionary? There is no earthly reason for pigeonholing them this way. Phonics is one way of teaching reading based on certain psychological and linguistic principles, and the word method is another way—based on certain other, inferior psychological principles and no linguistic principles whatever.

To be sure, it so happens that practically all progressive educators nowadays are also devotees of the word method. But that's simply a historical accident. It hasn't always been so and it isn't so today in other countries. Obviously there are liberal-minded teachers galore in England, Scotland, Wales, Scandinavia, France, and a dozen other countries, who swear by phonics and wouldn't think of teaching reading any other way. As to the past, progressive education hasn't always been wedded to the word method by any means. I cited earlier in this book the work of the famous Italian progressive kindergarten teacher, Dr. Maria Montessori. I could have cited similar statements by other patron saints of progressive education, like Pestalozzi and Froebel, or by Horace Mann, who observed the teaching of phonics in Prussia and recommended it enthusiastically for use in American schools.

What it comes down to, when you stop to analyze the philosophical underpinnings of the word-method gospel, is the repeated assertion that sight reading leads to joy and happiness in the classroom, playful, enthusiastic learning, "zest and zeal," a continuous glow of breathless excitement, and innumerable other priceless spiritual benefits. I ask you, soberly and sincerely, whether, according to your experience, that is true. Does all this really happen in classrooms or isn't this just a never-never land dreamed up by the educators? I certainly haven't seen any of this glorious joy and happiness on my visits to your school, and I can't believe that all those visits of mine happened to fall on off days. No, what I saw was the average class period, the thing that goes on in your classroom day by day. They learn the words, they read the "stories" in their readers. Some are happy, some are not, and most of them don't particularly feel one way or the other.

As to the "stories," *they* certainly are not calculated to arouse boundless enthusiasm in the soul of a child. I wonder who ever seriously thought of that curious notion. Has it ever happened to you that one of your children really got excited about "The Move to the Farm" and waited in breathless suspense to see what was going to happen next? I bet it hasn't. I can assure you that none of my own children ever came home from school and said, "Daddy, we read a *wonderful* story today in school. It was all about Dick and Jane's father stopping at a gas station."

Anyway, what can you expect of reading material cooked up

to contain 287 words, each repeated 26 times? Considering the circumstances, it's a wonder those readers are not considerably worse. Just imagine the poor writers, pressed into service to furnish those wretched little tales. All they *can* do is write something or other about that oh, so typical family with father, mother, a boy and a girl of primary-school age and a little sister. The little sister has a teddy bear. Father has a fairly good junior executive job and comes home from the office in a neat business suit. They live in a colonial house with a medium-sized yard and a white picket fence around it, about fifteen miles from a large metropolitan city equipped with a zoo and other facilities for children's reading material. They drive a Ford, Plymouth, or Chevrolet, and have grandparents devoted to a very rural type of farming with pigs, goats, geese, and the rest.

Naturally the children are bored—just as bored as you are yourself, reading their books with them day after day. The only way to give them some happiness and joy of achievement is to teach them phonics—the only system by which they'll arrive within reasonably short time at the pleasurable stage of being able to read anything they like. Interest and motivation —the great twin magics of progressive education—cannot be produced artificially by "story" after "story" about putting away toys or getting a new hat, but only by equipping the children with a skill that will help them in their own life. The other day a woman told me that her nine-year-old boy had finally taken an interest in reading because he wanted to decipher the television programs in the paper. There you have an example of real-life motivation.

To me, those artificial "stories" are in themselves proof that the word method is no good. A natural method of teaching reading should be usable anywhere, at any time, with whatever materials are at hand. The pioneers, as I mentioned before, managed with Webster's *Blue-Backed Speller* and the Bible. Innumerable people have managed with less—with the Bible alone, or just pencil and paper, plus a rudimentary knowledge of phonics. In fact, thousands of gifted children have learned to read by themselves, figuring out the basic sound values of certain letters and going on from there.

This primitive method of learning how to read is a great American tradition. Lincoln in his log cabin must have learned that way; so did his successor Andrew Johnson, the illiterate tailor's apprentice who taught himself to read when he was ten "from a book which contained selected orations of great British and American statesmen." Can you imagine a poor boy today who will educate himself by painstakingly working his way through the three Macmillan readers with their 1,278 words? I can't.

I am not dragging in Lincoln and Andrew Johnson gratuitously. There is a connection between phonics and democracy —a fundamental connection. Equal opportunity for all is one of the inalienable rights, and the word method interferes with that right.

You don't believe me? Think of the children in your class, think of the way you grouped them by their reading ability. There are three groups—aren't there?—the good readers, the average readers, and the poor readers. You know much better than I what are the exact "mental ages" or "reading ages" of those children. Isn't it true that you have a large group reading at the level that corresponds to your grade (that's the national norm I am talking about, two years behind the rest of the world), a somewhat smaller group reading one grade below, a still smaller group reading two grades below, and two or three or four poor Harrys who can't read at all? Yes, you also have a few children reading *above* your grade standard, but aren't they the exceptions? Isn't it true that in your class—and in any typical class—there is a cluster of children who are up to par in their reading, and a long, long comet's tail of children at all grade levels below, reaching all the way down to "non-readers"?

I know that educators take great pride in just that. We've

done away with rigid grade standards, they say, we now pay attention to individual differences in ability. We give each child in each class just as much as he can handle.

Frankly, when I first saw this tremendous variety of accomplishment in each classroom, I was shocked. I don't think at all that this is something to be proud of, I think it's deplorable. What's so wonderful about teaching twenty-five children at twenty-five different grade levels, mixed together in one classroom? How can anyone do an efficient teaching job in a third grade that contains Harry who can't tell the difference between *after* and *chasing?* The way I look at it, we're getting right back to the old-style one-room Little Red Schoolhouse, where the village teacher faced all the children in the community between the ages of six and twelve. Now we have shiny, sprawling new school buildings everywhere, and each of the classrooms is a miniature Little Red Schoolhouse open to children at all grade levels.

And where does this impossible situation come from? It comes directly from the word method—the method by which children are exposed to twelve hundred words in three years and left to learn to read by themselves. For reading, as I have said before, doesn't mean recognizing twelve hundred words by sight. It means being able to decipher and understand *any* word within one's vocabulary—and the vocabulary of an average college freshman, for instance, has been estimated by Seashore to be 158,000 words. How does a child or a teen-ager learn to read the 156,800 words he *hasn't* met in his three basic readers? There is only one way: he has to know something about phonics.

Since he isn't taught phonics in school, he has to get it from somewhere else. If he is a gifted child, he will gradually work out for himself which letter stands for which sound, and by doing that—and only by doing that—he will learn how to read. If, however, he is not the kind of child who figures things out for himself, he has to learn how to read at home, from his father and mother. By that I don't mean that his parents will teach him anything formally and systematically; of course they won't. But if they are educated people, if there are books and magazines in the home, if there is an atmosphere favorable to reading, the child will somehow, through his pores, learn the fundamental facts about English spelling that his school is denying him. He will ask his parents questions about words, and his parents will answer those questions. They will answer them invariably in terms of phonics and *never* in terms of the word method. They will not tell him that the word means *chipmunk* because "You remember the chipmunk in the story we read last month?" They'll tell him, naturally, "Look at the first two letters. What does *ch* stand for?"

And so reading, in so far as it is taught at all today, is taught, casually and unconsciously, by fathers and mothers at home. The child who comes from an educated, book-reading home has a tremendous advantage. The son of illiterate parents will stumble for three years through the twelve hundred words without help or guidance and then, as likely as not, develop into a "nonreader." An Andrew Johnson, with great gifts and perseverance, may still become President today; but the odds against him are now immeasurably greater.

I say, therefore, that the word method is gradually destroying democracy in this country; it returns to the upper middle class the privileges that public education was supposed to distribute evenly among the people. The American Dream is, essentially, equal opportunity through free education for all. This dream is beginning to vanish in a country where the public schools are falling down on the job.

It used to be the typical American ideal—and practice—to give children a better education than their parents had had. Fathers who never got beyond eighth grade sent their children to high school; high-school graduates proudly watched their sons getting college degrees. But things have changed in the last ten, twenty years. For the first time in history American parents see their children getting *less* education than they got themselves. Their sons and daughters come home from school and they can't read the newspaper; they can't spell simple words like *February* or *Wednesday;* they don't know the difference between Austria and Australia. The fathers and mothers don't know the reason for this, but they know that something terrible has happened to their most precious dreams and aspirations, that something, somewhere, is very, very wrong.

The educators, of course, deny that anything has happened. They trot out all sorts of data and statistics to show that American children read, write, and spell much better than they used to. I am not going to disprove those data one by one. What I am talking about here are not matters for argument but facts—facts that are public knowledge. The American people know what they know.

You are a grade-school teacher. I know that you are doing a conscientious job, that you work overtime for very little pay, that you love children and are proud of your profession. Aren't you getting tired of being attacked and criticized all the time? Every second mother who comes in to talk to you tells you that she is dissatisfied, that her child doesn't seem to learn anything, that you should do your job in a different way, that you don't know your business. Why should you be the scapegoat? The educators in their teachers' colleges and publishing offices think up all those fancy ideas, and you are on the firing line and have to take the consequences. Have another look at the system you are defending with so much effort. I know you are an intelligent young woman. You belong on the other side.

Mind you, I am not accusing the reading "experts" of wickedness or malice. I am not one of those people who call them un-American or left-wingers or Communist fellow travelers. All I am saying is that their theories are wrong and that the application of those theories has done untold harm to our younger generation.

Recently I saw some statistics that between 1945 and 1953,

33 million babies were born in this country. These children are now—or are soon going to be—in first, second, or third grade.

Let's forget about the past. Let's not argue about doctrines and theories, about who is to blame for what has happened.

Let's start all over again and do better by those 33 million.

EXERCISES

LIST OF EXERCISES

26 oo as in moon, book, and poor
27 ar   a as in pa, ma
28 or
29 er   ir   ur
30 oi   oy
31 ou   ow as in cow
32 au   aw   all   alt   alk
33 Review
34 ai   ay   air
35 ie as in pie   y as in by   ye as in rye   ind as in mind
          ild as in wild
36 oa   oe   old   olt   oll   ow as in low   o as in so
37 ew   ue
38 Review
39 Two-Syllable and Three-Syllable Words
40 a as in name
41 a as in name (continued)   a as in care   e as in Eve and
          here
42 i as in fine and fire
43 Review
44 o as in bone and more
45 Review
46 u as in tune and cure
47 Review
48 ing
49 y, ies, ied as in hurry, hurries, hurried
     y, ier, iest, ily as in happy, happier, happiest, happily
50 Review
51 ed
52 Review
53 er   le
54 Review
55 ce   ci   cy
56 ge   gi   gy   dge   dgi   dgy
57 Review

58   se, si, sy as in cheese, rising, rosy
     the, thi as in other, bathing
59   Review
60   Silent b, g, k, t, w
61   Silent gh, h, l
62   ph   gh as in rough
63   Review
64   Review
65   ea as in break, head, and learn
66   ie as in field   ui as in fruit   u as in put
67   wa   swa   wor   qua   squa   wha   ou as in young
            and famous
68   Review
69   ci, si, ti as in special, pension, vision, station, action
     su as in treasure   tu as in nature
70   ive as in active   or   ance   ence   come   some
71   Review
72   Three-Syllable and Four-Syllable Words

INSTRUCTIONS

1. Start with the sounds of the letters on pp. 142-146. Teach Johnny to make the sound when you point to the letter and to point to the letter or write the letter when you make the sound. The sound to be learned is always the beginning sound of the two words pictured.

Take as much time as seems necessary for this preliminary work; a five-year-old may well spend several weeks at it. Be patient: it will pay off later on. Don't aim for perfection. Rather, make sure Johnny realizes that letters stand for sounds and is reasonably good at connecting the right sound with the right letter.

Then, and only then, start Exercise 1.

2. Whenever Johnny is stumped by a word in the exercises, let him work it out for himself. Tell him to sound out the word. If he can't, let him look up the letter that is puzzling him on pp. 142-146, 156, 162, 168, or 170 and refresh his memory of its sound by naming the two pictures aloud. Let him do this as often as necessary until he is perfectly sure of the sound of the letter.

3. Explain to Johnny carefully that there is a small letter and a capital letter for each sound. However, concentrate on the small letters first. Difficulties with capital letters can be straightened out later.

4. Use the exercises to teach writing and spelling as well as reading. You will probably be tempted to go ahead with the reading and slight the writing and spelling. Try to resist that

temptation. Ideally, Johnny should learn to read and write each of the exercise words at the same time. Let him write each of the words from dictation. It is well worth taking the extra time.

5. There is a large amount of repetition in the exercises, and 22 of the 72 exercises are reviews. However, that doesn't mean that doing each exercise once is enough. Do each one of them until Johnny can read and write each word in it without the slightest hesitation. When you have done all the words horizontally, from left to right, do them vertically. Do them from right to left. Do them from the bottom up, diagonally, and picking words here and there at random. Make as sure as you can that Johnny can really read all the words.

6. Do the exercises in the exact order in which they are printed. Otherwise you'll defeat your purpose.

7. Watch out for signs of word guessing. Whenever Johnny does any guessing, insist on his sounding out the word and, if necessary, looking up the letter sounds on pp. 142-146, 156, 162, 168 or 170.

A a *A a*

APPLE

ARROW

E e *E e*

EGG

ELEPHANT

I i *I i*

INK

INDIAN

O o *O o*

OX

OSTRICH

U u *U u*

UMBRELLA

UNCLE SAM

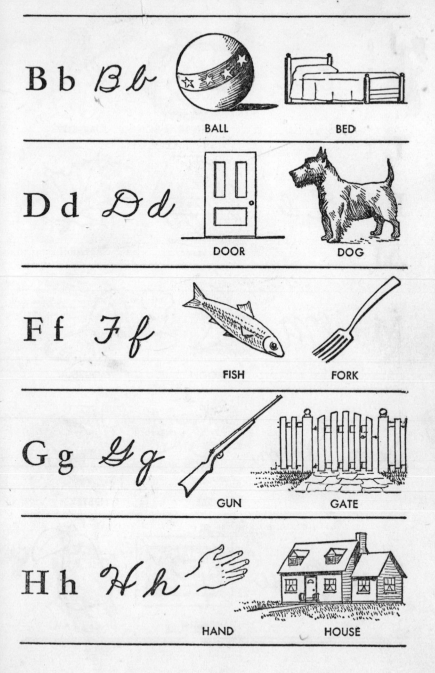

B b *Bb*	BALL	BED
D d *Dd*	DOOR	DOG
F f *Ff*	FISH	FORK
G g *Gg*	GUN	GATE
H h *Hh*	HAND	HOUSE

J j *J j*

JACK-IN-THE-BOX   JUMP-ROPE

L l *L l*

LAMP   LEAF

M m *M m*

MOON   MOUSE

N n *N n*

NOSE   NEST

P p *P p*

PICTURE   PEAR

R r *R r*

RING   ROSE

S s *S s*

SUN   SOLDIER

T t *T t*

TABLE   TENT

V v *V v*

VASE   VIOLIN

W w *W w*

WINDOW   WAGON

Y y *Y y*

YARD

YAWN

Z z *Z z*

ZEBRA

ZIPPER

1

mat	jam	rat	map	man
ham	Nat	pad	mad	Dan
fan	bag	wag	rag	sad
hag	fat	pat	tap	pan
map	lap	Sam	mass	dad
rap	tan	Pam	gas	Ann
bat	tag	fan	nap	mat
lap	Nat	pass	Sam	man
mad	tan	Dan	ham	bat
mass	pan	gas	rat	bag
jazz	tap	wag	Ann	pad
pat	rag	fat	map	Pam
tag	jam	sad	rap	dad
had	sad	dad	van	tap
wag	jam	hag	nap	fan
ham	rap	map	tan	van
pass	mass	mat	Ann	pad
lap	Dan	rat	fat	pat

2

e

yes	men	tell	egg	net
pen	bet	bell	let	pen
net	sell	bed	get	den
den	leg	yes	bet	leg
pet	Ben	web	well	red
get	bed	hen	sell	Ben
Ned	jet	less	yell	mess
hen	wet	Ben	yet	Ed
set	less	Ned	wet	egg
men	web	ten	pen	wet
tell	ten	Ted	sell	yes
bell	beg	mess	pet	men
Ted	well	den	peg	let
mess	yell	set	red	tell
Ed	pet	leg	Ted	Ned
let	red	Ed	bed	bet
peg	net	men	web	less
red	peg	beg	egg	yes

3

Review

sad	ten	Ann	bed	mat
pass	tag	rap	leg	mess
Ted	less	gas	web	Pam
Ed	yell	fat	bet	dad
pad	Dan	tap	let	lap
Ned	yes	rat	Sam	sell
man	map	peg	well	red
hen	pat	wag	net	mass
jet	jam	pan	pet	den
fan	wet	hag	tan	Ben
ham	bat	jazz	egg	rag
get	set	tell	nap	yet
mad	bag	pen	men	beg
egg	get	yet	mass	Nat
pet	rat	bell	pat	hen
pad	hag	web	men	mat
fat	well	wet	less	fan
leg	map	bag	yell	gas

4

i

miss	fit	did	Jim	Jill
Sis	nip	fib	dig	bib
bit	him	sit	hip	hit
sin	sip	Bill	fig	win
rip	Tim	bin	hill	pin
will	mill	zip	dip	wig
tip	lid	big	pig	lip
fill	rib	sip	dip	bit
sit	pig	hit	nip	fig
lip	fit	dig	Bill	Jim
lid	him	pin	sin	Sis
rip	hill	did	win	hip
wig	fill	Jill	tip	bin
mill	rib	Tim	miss	will
zip	fig	big	sip	lip
sin	Bill	bib	win	bit
Tim	Jill	rib	rip	will
lid	him	nip	fib	Sis

5

Review

leg	Tim	jam	Ben	dad
fib	Ann	bin	fat	yes
bat	lip	rag	yet	wag
red	mad	man	nip	pat
tan	tell	web	get	beg
bet	less	Ted	zip	Jill
men	rat	lap	hen	map
yell	win	Dan	hag	Sis
tap	miss	sip	mat	Sam
let	fill	Ned	pad	Pam
mill	Jim	bin	set	peg
Ed	jazz	will	mess	fit
pig	gas	sad	pass	ten
tag	hip	dip	net	tip
rip	sin	fan	him	lid
Bill	well	wet	ham	den
hill	bag	wig	rap	nap
pet	bib	sell	bed	did

6

o

nod	God	sob	dot	pop
not	boss	hot	moss	log
doll	lot	pot	hop	Bob
got	top	job	hog	dog
Tom	fog	mop	Don	rob
God	Don	lot	sob	pot
hog	fog	boss	dog	rob
not	job	moss	nod	Tom
got	dot	mop	top	pop
Bob	hot	hop	doll	log
Tom	fog	nod	dot	boss
log	mop	hot	rob	hog
not	got	God	moss	doll
job	pop	pot	Bob	top
Don	nod	sob	dog	lot
Bob	Tom	nod	top	dot
fog	boss	God	moss	pop
not	log	sob	Don	dog

7

Review

sit	Don	pin	fat	mop
ham	lip	fan	Ted	him
rap	nap	pen	hit	pet
lid	pot	fib	hag	let
zip	bin	dog	pop	van
Bill	Jim	bib	fill	well
hog	pat	jam	tag	Sis
yet	hop	yell	sob	bag
Ned	lot	rob	rat	log
Ben	did	rib	fit	Nat
set	yes	mess	hot	mad
moss	Dan	lap	fig	miss
bed	sip	hip	Ann	bit
wig	top	fog	job	pad
tan	mass	tell	Jill	red
hen	will	boss	bell	jazz
men	web	dig	wag	net
Pam	got	dip	den	tip

8

u

hum	run	bus	bug	tug
nun	bud	sun	sum	bun
mutt	tub	huff	pup	fuzz
nut	mug	mud	hut	Gus
hug	rub	rug	gun	muff
but	fuss	dull	fun	gum
hut	rug	gum	sun	rub
dull	run	bus	pup	bug
fun	sum	hug	nut	but
puff	mug	bun	fuss	mud
buzz	gun	hum	tug	tub
nun	Gus	muff	bud	huff
tub	mutt	bun	but	hug
gum	gun	run	bug	mutt
dull	mug	rug	pup	sum
bus	tug	nut	hum	nun
fuss	Gus	sun	fun	hut
puff	fuzz	mud	rub	bud

9

Review

dig	wig	bed	moss	egg
pass	mud	hit	dad	hot
men	rob	set	hop	fun
mass	Tim	web	Dan	buzz
top	bet	hug	map	dip
tell	pan	lid	pet	boss
big	rip	rib	hen	nip
fuss	but	nap	sip	bell
fill	mug	muff	jazz	let
Jill	pad	fog	bit	rat
Ned	fig	mill	hum	pat
beg	got	sell	fib	sum
jam	tip	sob	doll	fuzz
Ann	dog	pup	Ed	Bob
Nat	Ted	well	bib	yet
win	net	Gus	wet	tug
gas	den	ten	jet	lip
yell	nod	tap	hip	tan

C c *C c*

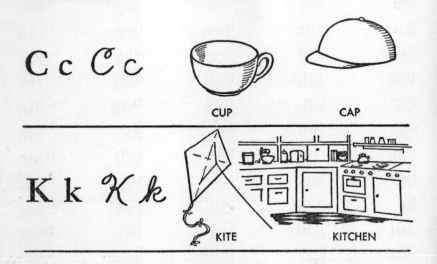

CUP   CAP

K k *K k*

KITE   KITCHEN

10

c k

can	cat	cut	cap	cod
kiss	cuff	cup	cop	cab
cub	kill	cot	keg	kit
kid	cab	cuff	can	cut
cob	cap	cub	cup	kiss
kill	cat	keg	kit	kid
cop	cod	cot	kill	kiss
cat	cuff	cod	keg	kit
kid	cob	cap	cab	cut
can	cup	cot	cub	cap
cuff	cob	cat	cop	cot
can	cut	kiss	cup	keg
kit	cub	cab	cod	cub
kill	kid	cot	cap	cuff
cob	cod	cub	kill	cot
can	cut	kiss	cup	cat
keg	kit	cop	kid	kit
cup	cab	cat	cut	cod

11

ck

pick	tick	luck	lick	suck
lock	lack	kick	sick	pack
tack	Dick	neck	tuck	buck
buck	rack	deck	sock	rock
Nick	hack	dock	Jack	back
sack	duck	luck	sack	Dick
Nick	pack	back	duck	tuck
tick	pick	dock	rack	sick
buck	lock	neck	deck	lick
Dick	sock	kick	Jack	tack
rock	hack	suck	lack	lock
tick	sick	rock	dock	hack
buck	lick	deck	Dick	neck
luck	sack	pack	duck	pick
back	deck	Nick	tuck	sock
lock	suck	rack	Jack	tack
kick	luck	duck	tick	Dick
dock	deck	lack	sack	rack

12

Review

sum	deck	sack	him	lock
Tim	cap	can	bet	puff
cut	cob	back	rock	set
hop	dad	rack	fun	kill
suck	cod	jet	hot	dock
lick	web	van	men	red
cat	kick	tuck	moss	rob
pad	luck	top	mass	cop
let	Dick	kid	egg	fib
ten	log	Jack	sick	rock
cub	Tom	fuzz	dig	wig
pick	pass	zip	Jill	kit
cuff	tick	kiss	bed	hack
sack	cup	cab	lip	mud
duck	tack	pack	Nick	keg
neck	lack	hit	buck	mess
pad	lock	bed	red	cuff
set	back	sick	yell	duck

13

ct ft lb lf lk lm lp lt mp nd nt pt sk sp st

nest	best	dump	mend	rest
land	belt	bond	bend	lend
test	vest	limp	bulb	hump
kept	ask	just	band	hint
desk	pond	went	zest	self
fist	dust	rust	pest	camp
mist	fact	list	hunt	lump
bent	gift	milk	sift	felt
fond	left	must	lift	end
west	gulp	help	wept	silk
lent	last	fast	melt	sulk
elf	bulk	lisp	pump	bump
sand	send	tent	mint	lamp
dusk	jump	damp	mist	dusk
zest	fond	bulb	mask	lisp
jump	desk	list	last	melt
fist	lump	rest	camp	must
sulk	and	ask	help	send

14

bs cks ds ffs gs lls ms ns ps ts cts fts lbs
lks lms lps lts mps nds nts pts sks sps sts

cats	lifts	digs	asks	ribs
tops	cuts	mends	tubs	mats
rests	hens	sips	masks	hints
jumps	bats	cups	melts	pants
beds	pumps	sells	pigs	elms
milks	camps	gulps	hops	cuffs
gifts	facts	wigs	cops	fins
pills	acts	hums	bugs	ducks
helps	lisps	hands	bills	dusts
rips	hills	guns	sulks	nests
cuffs	sips	ducks	buns	tops
pumps	hills	tubs	fins	acts
sulks	jumps	lips	cuts	helps
facts	hats	wigs	bills	hands
hens	bats	rips	hops	bugs
gifts	cats	cups	elms	ribs
dusts	beds	digs	sells	pigs
masks	cops	pants	lifts	mends

Sh sh *Sh sh*

SHOE   SHADOW

15

ng   nk   sh   x   ngs   nks

hash	pink	rush	hang	sink
ink	gash	bank	ax	sunk
next	dash	box	wing	ox
dunk	sing	cash	ash	gush
tax	link	fix	fish	mash
long	Max	monk	dish	rung
song	wax	gang	ring	tank
winks	lungs	junk	lash	bangs
mink	sash	wish	six	mush
ox	hush	rash	mix	fox
hash	rank	tax	sash	wish
mix	hang	king	wing	junk
bangs	lungs	gash	bank	sing
wax	Max	next	six	fix
rash	dash	ox	mash	lash
rung	song	pink	gang	cash
rush	tank	bank	monk	ink
ax	ash	winks	dunk	link

163

16

Review

wax	dish	left	gifts	fond
nests	box	sulks	cuffs	rung
ribs	dusts	elf	bulb	sash
hunt	bills	mint	last	bangs
cash	bulk	facts	six	fish
ash	sand	lump	hush	vest
sunk	Max	mush	hats	wigs
wish	mats	lamp	desk	tent
dust	hands	dusk	zest	sulks
milk	best	winks	kept	lift
next	mix	long	cats	rest
pest	ducks	hints	gulps	fox
land	belt	lend	beds	sells
dunk	digs	jumps	ponds	camp
tank	pills	hint	fix	sunk
rush	test	hang	melt	mash
ask	rips	lungs	hump	bent
gang	acts	list	ax	west

17

bl cl fl gl pl sc sk sl sm sn sp st sw tw spl

lump—plump	tub—stub	lap—flap
lamp—clamp	win—twin	lad—glad
lip—clip	pan—span	lock—block
lend—blend	lack—slack	lint—splint
camp—scamp	well—swell	nap—snap
lap—clap	pit—spit	lip—slip
link—blink	lash—splash	lock—flock
pick—spick	wept—swept	lash—flash
pill—spill	lip—flip	lick—slick

snip	blink	clap	stem	slink
twin	spick	plum	clamp	click
block	plot	club	stab	slap
glad	clump	snag	splash	stop
stub	blend	slip	clip	flag
flop	flap	twig	skip	swell
swim	slick	spit	flash	stick
slot	span	scat	plum	snap
slack	flint	swig	flock	glint

18

br cr dr fr gr pr scr spr str shr tr

rat—brat	rub—scrub		rip—grip	
ring—bring	rink—drink		rag—brag	
rust—crust	rip—strip		rim—brim	
rip—trip	rug—drug		ramp—cramp	
rust—trust	rap—strap		ring—string	
rash—crash	rush—brush		rug—shrug	
brim	frank	brush	shrimp	spring
grill	drank	grand	grip	brat
brink	strap	trot	crest	brand
drink	bring	prompt	crust	trust
Fred	frog	drug	shrug	drill
cramp	tramp	drum	truck	prank
print	crack	crash	strip	grunt
drink	crush	grin	string	trap
crock	fresh	crank	dress	press
frills	Fran	drip	scrub	shrub
frock	crust	strong	brisk	trick
shrug	cramp	drab	crab	strip

19

Review

jump	rush	sulks	pump	stop
self	vest	send	bend	frill
mends	digs	plot	brand	skip
rest	lift	pest	belt	winks
drum	mist	fact	sells	Fran
jumps	must	test	dash	stub
stem	crash	buns	kept	ring
lips	ox	mend	scrub	sled
step	trust	flash	bats	tops
tank	skip	hints	gulps	fox
gift	bugs	flock	dump	melts
truck	scamp	strip	swim	spring
bump	tent	drift	sash	help
sing	hunt	grip	grill	drank
crash	bent	bills	mint	brat
gang	press	dust	stick	sunk
hands	hums	acts	crib	blend
limp	song	glad	Max	mush

Qu qu *Qu qu*

QUEEN QUARTER

Th th *Th th*

THORN THISTLE

Wh wh *Wh wh*

WHIP WHEEL

20

smith	whip	whack	thin	quiz
this	think	then	thick	quill
with	broth	thrush	thrift	quack
squint	thrash	thrill	when	whisk
that	whiff	cloth	them	quick
quit	whim	quilt	thump	thank
then	when	whiff	quilt	moth
quick	smith	quiz	them	thrash
this	broth	whack	quack	quit
squint	whip	whim	quill	thank
thick	thrill	that	whisk	thin
with	moth	thing	thrush	thump
think	thrift	cloth	smith	broth
with	whim	quill	them	thrill
then	when	that	whip	quack
thrush	thing	whiff	thump	think
thrift	quiz	thank	whisk	thick
whack	cloth	whip	quit	quick

Ch ch *Ch ch*

CHAIR   CHAIN

21

ch tch

chum	witch	chunk	chin	chill
pinch	clutch	chest	punch	branch
stretch	crutch	chick	stitch	which
much	patch	pitch	fetch	latch
trench	check	itch	hitch	bunch
lunch	sketch	notch	chink	crunch
ditch	ranch	chat	such	bench
quench	catch	match	chop	chap
hunch	snatch	clinch	rich	stitch
switch	check	chick	such	bench
notch	ditch	stitch	which	hunch
quench	witch	much	snatch	clutch
punch	pinch	hitch	stretch	lunch
ranch	bunch	crutch	chest	chat
clinch	trench	latch	pitch	itch
branch	catch	stitch	chap	chum
chunk	fetch	chink	switch	crunch
chin	chop	chill	match	patch

22

Review

kept	thrill	monk	scat	quench
ring	step	jumps	switch	sketch
notch	chunk	bugs	chick	patch
crack	flap	ash	wax	moth
thrash	mush	stop	sing	slip
test	trip	grunt	hunt	grip
chink	clip	camp	chop	hints
glad	ask	sand	branch	damp
pond	brat	gang	hills	flint
slot	milk	ink	facts	lifts
tax	bangs	spit	lend	dash
stub	masks	cuffs	hops	strip
fins	frog	much	mist	crib
clamp	drunk	mink	chick	that
whisk	block	bump	shrub	nest
melt	punch	sled	gulps	long
clap	strap	dress	drift	brink
prompt	mend	wept	snag	lumps

23

Two-Syllable Words

address	hatbox	fishpond	stocking
bucket	exit	longest	ringlet
mustang	bathtub	slipper	crossing
unfit	dustpan	sunset	vivid
quicksand	shopping	upset	tinsmith
kitchen	dishpan	biggest	hatrack
lobster	tomcat	mastiff	spirit
privet	lapdog	padlock	dangling
buckskin	topnotch	handbag	bellhop
hamster	mistress	blister	dentist
winter	goblin	wicked	robin
locket	chicken	rabbit	napkin
lemon	frosting	redskin	basket
vanish	blinker	whiskers	chipmunk
catnip	tempest	lipstick	sunset
dustpan	crossing	bathtub	vivid
shopping	tinsmith	tomcat	dangling
lemon	quicksand	goblin	napkin
slipper	blinker	lapdog	rabbit
biggest	chicken	zipper	blister

24

ee   ea as in meal   e as in he

steel—steal		seem—seam		meet—meat
peel—peal		peek—peak		week—weak
deer—dear		flee—flea		teem—team
zeal	leap	feet	sheet	peep
be	cheat	beach	beast	steer
preach	cheap	wheel	reach	beam
seek	deep	heap	sweep	sheer
east	lean	weep	sweet	weed
gear	creep	teach	bean	peach
fear	neat	we	speak	seen
street	spear	seed	squeak	ear
queen	clear	tree	free	leaf
feel	reap	tea	scream	bead
steam	stream	bees	yeast	need
wheat	near	keel	three	hear
speech	me	heat	beak	queer
seat	feed	green	sheep	veal
year	screen	dream	seal	keep

25

ee	ea as in meal	e as in he		
each	she	meek	creep	he
beer	squeal	deal	steep	cream
deed	mean	sleep	fleet	speed
peas	Jean	cheek	treat	eat
heal	feet	keep	feed	beak
queer	each	bead	queen	clear
tree	steer	preach	zeal	speed
reap	peas	tea	be	we
speak	free	meat	mean	speech
need	beets	cheat	lean	weep
keen	leap	dream	green	treat
seen	leaf	she	meek	beam
screen	seek	beer	sheet	near
beef	beach	street	sweet	yeast
bean	sleep	spear	seed	feel
reed	sheep	weeds	gear	scream
creep	teach	see	peach	breed
veal	stream	steam	me	heat

26

oo as in moon, book, and poor

broom	drool	soot	cool	spoon
moo	loop	tool	took	coop
roof	troop	crook	boost	too
stoop	brood	shook	hood	tooth
wood	hook	food	look	booth
mood	coo	moon	stood	room
spool	cook	fool	noon	snoop
soon	wool	stool	boom	shoot
hoop	droop	nook	spook	scoop
good	smooth	book	bloom	foot
hoof	root	poor	zoo	pool
boot	good	hood	coop	broom
stood	loop	foot	food	took
coo	hook	hoop	drool	smooth
fool	stool	stoop	spool	pool
booth	boot	spoon	too	tooth
droop	wood	book	scoop	root
troop	brood	nook	tool	hoof

27

ar   a as in pa, ma

yard	park	smart	starch	lard
sharp	start	darn	car	lark
art	scarf	barn	harm	pa
bar	star	jar	dark	spark
card	bark	scar	charm	lark
ma	shark	march	ark	part
marsh	dart	arm	yarn	cart
far	mark	hard	tar	chart
farm	arch	harp	Carl	bar
darn	hard	yard	bark	Carl
start	march	mark	starch	ma
arch	tar	park	pa	car
card	marsh	jar	harm	dart
star	ark	chart	art	charm
farm	shark	harp	scarf	barn
lard	arm	yarn	smart	dark
cart	far	part	lark	bark
scar	spark	sharp	chart	car

28

or

storm	scorch	porch	corn	lord
north	torn	form	for	thorn
scorn	fort	cork	sort	port
cord	short	or	sworn	born
torch	horn	sport	snort	fork
pork	sort	worn	stork	form
corn	for	short	north	port
worn	horn	fork	sport	cord
sworn	sort	stork	born	porch
or	cork	pork	storm	short
lord	scorch	fort	torch	thorn
scorn	snort	torn	born	stork
for	storm	or	corn	snort
lord	cork	torn	fort	sworn
short	pork	scorch	porch	sort
scorn	fork	form	sport	port
north	cord	worn	torch	horn
thorn	fork	form	north	torch

29

sir	birth	fir	burn	birch
shirt	thirst	dirt	bird	stir
jerk	curb	surf	chirp	fur
girl	whirl	skirt	purr	churn
clerk	squirm	burst	hurt	third
hers	turn	curl	hurl	shirk
Bert	first	burr	church	squirt
firm	twirl	perch	stern	fern
herd	her	furl	spur	Bert
hurt	bird	whirl	birth	stir
furl	curl	clerk	skirt	herd
fir	jerk	churn	sir	firm
third	chirp	fur	shirt	girl
stern	burn	squirt	curb	hers
dirt	burr	church	twirl	birch
turn	perch	shirk	thirst	her
firm	burst	surf	purr	hurl
spur	squirm	first	furl	perch

30

oi   oy

point	boy	join	foil	joy
hoist	broil	coy	Roy	soil
spoil	loin	toil	coil	boil
oil	toys	moist	joint	cloy
spoil	coy	loin	hoist	foist
foil	joint	broil	boil	point
toys	coil	join	coin	moist
coy	soil	point	boy	toil
joy	Roy	oil	coy	join
broil	moist	spoil	Roy	point
soil	joint	foil	boil	toil
coy	toys	coil	foist	cloy
loin	coin	joy	hoist	toil
broil	soil	moist	boil	hoist
join	loin	spoil	foil	toys
boy	coin	coy	joint	joy
cloy	Roy	oil	coil	point
coy	oil	boil	hoist	coin

31

ou   ow as in cow

sound	growl	how	owl	count
gown	pound	scout	bound	out
down	howl	grouch	found	now
cow	crouch	pout	stout	cloud
town	clown	fowl	crown	drown
foul	snout	brown	sprout	mouth
ground	loud	our	sour	trout
flour	spout	frown	hound	south
proud	couch	round	shout	pouch
spout	scout	cow	sprout	clown
couch	ground	ouch	pound	owl
sour	fowl	crown	hound	drown
snout	found	crouch	howl	out
now	growl	shout	brown	count
bound	gown	cloud	frown	proud
how	south	fowl	mouth	town
round	flour	trout	loud	our
grouch	sound	stout	pouch	pout

32

au   aw   all   alt   alk

jaw	hall	shawl	launch	stall
haul	halt	wall	flaw	all
bawl	call	taunt	brawl	straw
yawn	squall	saw	talk	fraud
thaw	sprawl	small	lawn	fall
law	malt	dawn	salt	hawk
stalk	Walt	fault	raw	bald
drawn	claw	chalk	tall	ball
paw	walk	crawl	Paul	draw
fall	ball	hall	small	malt
lawn	call	salt	brawl	jaw
flaw	halt	shawl	paw	stalk
Paul	thaw	all	squall	draw
raw	bald	claw	taunt	launch
sprawl	Walt	straw	walk	saw
haul	stall	fault	crawl	yawn
wall	dawn	law	talk	drawn
fraud	bawl	tall	hawk	chalk

33

Review

boom	cloud	squeal	torn	pout
steam	storm	or	down	spook
frown	reap	fort	our	sheep
toil	moist	chart	hound	wheat
week	wall	near	talk	cool
drown	broil	proud	soot	fear
salt	curl	lark	spout	boost
fault	thaw	jar	ouch	sweet
gown	ball	ground	how	beam
seek	charm	veal	street	loin
joy	peach	roof	draw	paw
bloom	found	brawl	farm	chirp
jaw	lord	ma	cork	shark
fur	bound	launch	for	crook
march	stir	Roy	bar	join
booth	foil	girl	fir	beach
moon	leaf	beast	Paul	star
arch	birch	drawn	coo	snout

34

ai ay air

aim	wait	jail	saint	tail
lay	pay	strain	quaint	plain
mail	hail	slay	bait	fail
snail	rail	paid	gray	sail
may	bay	trail	play	faint
pain	raid	braid	grain	clay
chain	way	fair	pail	spray
rain	gain	Cain	pray	stairs
day	stray	gay	brain	train
air	jay	drain	frail	pair
hair	quail	ray	faith	main
spray	aim	maid	chair	tray
chain	bray	paint	lair	stay
say	hay	fail	wail	stain
vain	sway	faith	say	mail
saint	may	bay	chair	braid
aim	tail	maid	pain	train
grain	clay	quaint	gain	lay

35

ie as in pie	y as in by	ye as in rye	ind as in mind
		ild as in wild	

cry	rind	flies	rye	tried
blind	die	mild	sly	find
why	died	try	fly	tie
mind	lies	bind	lie	my
kind	sky	fry	tied	by
blind	dried	dry	wild	child
pie	spy	shy	grind	fried
die	cries	rind	die	cry
child	try	by	tie	my
die	died	bind	lie	sky
grind	kind	dried	dry	mild
flies	fried	tried	rye	tied
find	fly	mind	lies	spy
why	sly	blind	cries	fry
shy	pie	wild	dry	why
died	dried	lies	sky	bind
child	fly	fried	grind	try
by	mild	tried	kind	find

36

blow	toll	coach	road	soap
mow	hoe	toad	bolt	old
blown	Joe	boat	float	told
cold	oak	goes	snow	coat
loan	grow	goat	load	woe
goal	whoa	soar	croak	oar
roast	foam	throw	groan	doe
loaf	grown	crow	colt	row
shown	coast	coal	stroll	sold
go	jolt	oath	no	gold
slow	bold	coax	flow	bowl
toe	so	scold	fold	toast
glow	oats	show	boast	foe
throat	roam	growth	soak	hold
low	roar	roast	foam	coach
boat	roll	blow	whoa	tow
cold	bolt	slow	load	glow
old	row	scroll	boast	loaf

37

ew   ue

blue	new	drew	glue	chew
stew	strew	crew	cue	threw
true	slew	Sue	due	dew
blew	flue	pew	Jew	hue
flew	screw	strewn	brew	flew
news	Sue	crew	strew	true
new	flue	glue	strewn	hue
flew	brew	pew	stew	drew
news	cue	blue	due	threw
Jew	chew	flew	dew	screw
blew	slew	Sue	threw	glue
clew	true	brew	Jew	drew
crew	strew	new	flue	pew
strewn	dew	hue	due	slew
chew	blew	flew	screw	flew
strew	news	blue	cue	blew
strewn	strew	hue	flew	glue
flue	news	brew	drew	stew

187

38

Review

snort	bay	soak	boil	herd
colt	hoe	tail	main	churn
spear	toe	coal	snow	scorch
porch	stroll	coat	mind	shy
sail	south	cry	say	spoil
beer	sleep	art	pa	shirk
cloy	mow	toast	soon	blind
neat	Bert	train	roar	broom
grain	droop	stoop	halt	brain
drew	wild	quaint	point	he
weed	squall	news	throat	jolt
thirst	throw	out	lies	sold
twirl	hard	keel	owl	woe
bark	Walt	chain	bait	roach
stall	tar	find	may	coin
trout	hall	Carl	stood	flew
boot	doe	grow	malt	roll
count	hear	bald	fowl	taunt

39

Two-Syllable and Three-Syllable Words

snowball	complain	reply	yellow
herself	around	shadow	November
Columbus	raincoat	pardon	leapfrog
agreement	seaport	teaspoon	flowers
punishment	borrow	sunbeam	butterfly
yesterday	classroom	booklet	tower
Thursday	September	banjo	smartest
Tuesday	gardener	electric	repeat
hamburger	mailbox	return	untrue
showers	always	Jefferson	toaster
awnings	away	confess	Saturday
cartoon	steamboat	counter	goodness
discover	numbers	Eskimo	understand
scarlet	jeweler	shortest	sheepish
oatmeal	swallow	Sunday	birthday
enjoyment	Herbert	New York	Mexico
murderer	railroad	annoy	August
western	Easter	lantern	burglar
window	belongs	kangaroo	mustard
unties	widow	Monday	seagull

40

a as in name

cap—cape		past—paste		gap—gape	
rat—rate		pan—pane		back—bake	
fad—fade		Sam—same		mad—made	
lack—lake		snack—snake		quack—quake	
at—ate		hat—hate		tap—tape	
cape	fake	tape	take	gaze
slate	shame	haste	mane	gate
trade	safe	make	made	ape
late	skate	plate	Dave	lame
hate	name	fade	Jane	rate
drape	waste	fate	game	sale
stale	pane	blaze	ate	Kate
plane	bake	wave	chase	rake
pave	slave	snake	flake	cake
tame	shave	taste	haze	state
daze	male	cane	spade	shake
came	grave	blade	cave	slate
brave	gate	blame	plate	crate

41

care	fare	square	dare	scare
snare	hare	rare	blare	stare
mare	share	glare	spare	flare
Pete	Eve	here	Steve	Eve
sane	frame	gaze	date	case
tale	mare	Pete	flame	lane
gale	rare	mate	pave	share
cake	Steve	tame	name	spare
wade	cave	rake	haste	grape
fare	Eve	same	base	hare
male	came	here	pane	sale
flake	frame	grate	save	wake
pane	hate	square	Jane	safe
Pete	bare	skate	same	ape
spade	glade	glare	shave	stare
lame	Kate	tape	grade	shame
game	share	Steve	gaze	base
lake	slate	snare	cape	Eve

42

i as in fine and fire

pin—pine		rip—ripe		win—wine	
lick—like		Tim—time		dim—dime	
shin—shine		spin—spine		kit—kite	
bit—bite		fill—file		rid—ride	
mill—mile		sit—site		Dick—dike	
wide	strike	tile	swipe		bite
size	ride	kite	bike		live
swine	fire	spike	like		ripe
time	hire	mine	glide		tide
rime	smile	pipe	Mike		while
spite	side	five	drive		dine
pride	site	mile	wife		prize
tire	dive	wine	life		hive
chime	quite	pile	pike		fine
stripe	dike	whine	spine		white
lime	glide	file	crime		wire
bride	vine	slide	stride		spite
hide	gripe	line	quite		smile

43

Review

cake	fine	cape	blaze	gate
hike	fake	shade	flake	mine
slave	mane	fare	drape	fade
time	sane	tale	lane	glide
care	gaze	lime	bite	dine
pike	quake	whale	shine	stare
while	hide	came	glide	pride
fare	plane	pipe	hive	whine
stripe	file	here	tape	Pete
Mike	line	dive	smile	gave
site	shame	ape	ride	wade
pine	frame	prize	kite	share
lame	plate	white	dike	vine
chase	hive	trade	five	bake
spite	tire	crime	case	tide
waste	wide	wife	shave	haste
rare	Eve	like	daze	Kate
Steve	flame	snake	drive	lake

44

o as in bone and more

not—note   cop—cope   mop—mope
rob—robe   smock—smoke   hop—hope

note	drove	choke	core	poke
mope	chore	sore	scope	stone
vote	stove	slope	rope	mole
robe	throne	score	broke	Rome
stole	smoke	froze	grove	doze
tone	grope	cope	hope	pole
lobe	snore	joke	sole	dote
hole	bone	store	dome	spoke
globe	cone	stroke	coke	more
shore	woke	rode	scope	throne
poke	store	stone	vote	hope
sole	mope	woke	doze	dome
rope	cope	score	joke	spoke
more	tone	stroke	pole	cone
snore	stole	core	stone	sore
slope	froze	chore	grope	wore

45

Review

shine	fire	paste	Jane	made
gale	broke	grate	tile	quite
grope	grave	Rome	smoke	spire
life	bride	tame	size	score
note	chime	male	gape	save
hide	base	make	spine	blade
date	pave	safe	hike	hole
robe	shore	dote	name	mare
late	drove	grove	sale	globe
bone	haze	bike	swine	grape
twine	game	spike	wine	take
dime	taste	slide	cane	slate
tame	skate	grade	rode	dare
strike	swipe	rake	glide	pile
glare	coke	wave	lobc	choke
mate	Dave	square	mole	spade
chore	scope	throne	cake	poke
cone	cape	line	pine	vine

46

u as in tune and cure

cut—cute		tub—tube	us—use	
purr—pure		duck—duke	cub—cube	
June	mule	flute	nude	crude
cute	prune	mute	Luke	pure
duke	tune	Rube	cure	rule
rude	cube	fluke	tube	brute
use	Rube	flute	lute	cube
pure	Luke	cute	June	mule
use	mute	brute	crude	cure
rule	rude	prune	tube	duke
nude	tune	use	flute	tube
cure	cube	cute	nude	mute
Rube	June	fluke	tune	rule
mule	rude	pure	brute	prune
Luke	crude	duke	mule	brute
crude	nude	Luke	cube	tube
duke	cure	prune	fluke	flute
lute	mule	pure	rule	tune

47

Review

wake	name	cane	pole	Rube
base	rude	quake	make	lane
drove	haste	slave	cure	spine
blade	whine	globe	shave	file
cone	fate	side	sore	cape
state	store	tone	prize	stone
mine	use	tube	drive	gaze
stove	froze	dime	pane	glide
site	swipe	pike	tame	pride
cave	late	cute	date	line
wide	fare	lame	pile	glare
pine	shine	coke	kite	shade
stale	ripe	sane	cube	came
grove	pave	chase	safe	fluke
live	core	fine	hive	waste
whale	snore	vine	hole	robe
lobe	haze	fire	rake	Luke
rope	mope	case	rime	tune

48

ing

hoping—hopping
filing—filling

scraping—scrapping
liking—licking

shopping	lining	setting	bedding
stirring	letting	rating	fibbing
dipping	shipping	sobbing	trimming
sagging	brimming	fitting	budding
drumming	spinning	sledding	slipping
betting	dipping	skimming	rubbing
purring	whipping	spelling	begging
grabbing	skipping	sipping	gazing
digging	hugging	running	shutting
fading	quitting	tipping	sitting
skipping	whipping	stirring	sledding
licking	dining	scraping	filing
topping	hoping	stabbing	fibbing
caring	grating	raving	dabbing
nagging	padding	canning	firing
tugging	sliding	wiping	whipping
sharing	buzzing	spinning	taping
naming	aping	stunning	grabbing

49

y, ies, ied as in hurry, hurries, hurried
y, ier, iest, ily as in happy, happier, happiest, happily

candy—candies   story—stories
fairy—fairies   pony—ponies
berry—berries   baby—babies
party—parties   lady—ladies
carry—carries—carried   hurry—hurries—hurried
happy—happier—happiest—happily
funny—funnier—funniest—funnily

fifty	nutty	witty	Betty
daddy	sadly	silliest	muddy
Billy	twenty	Peggy	scurried
chillier	ugly	navy	sunniest
forty	jury	thirty	hardly
Bobby	foggy	carried	dizzy
nearly	ladies	thirsty	dirtiest
sleepily	gladly	handily	candies
sixty	shady	roomier	bodies
hurries	likely	uglier	party
Peggy	fussy	Mary	penny
ivy	cozy	daily	snappy
gravy	bunny	puppies	kitty

50

Review

gladly	dizzy	bodies	whipping
skipping	fifty	filling	bedding
varied	brimming	budding	buggy
hurries	Mary	trimming	Betty
grabbing	wiping	Peggy	sandy
dipping	juries	fading	lazily
stirring	begging	fairies	slipping
silly	napping	letting	chillier
bunnies	badly	shortly	ugliest
hungrier	muddy	ferried	empty
Jimmy	fibbing	daddy	scrappy
setting	rubbing	sledding	counties
hopping	sobbing	digging	running
staring	sadly	crazy	puppies
married	foggy	navy	filing
thirty	candies	Billy	hugging
parties	wittily	pony	berries
fitting	messy	lady	dandy
matting	paring	cutting	fishy
sixty	armies	cherries	jelly

51

ed

robbed	matted	rested	added
blessed	boiled	stacked	stopped
hitched	wiped	helped	parked
sailed	buzzed	wheeled	fished
scratched	dropped	snapped	hissed
charmed	jumped	tipped	hushed
crawled	rugged	mixed	trapped
seated	cracked	patched	counted
jerked	canned	pinned	trailed
followed	spotted	leaped	skipped
filled	growled	slammed	stuffed
pinched	matched	fixed	scuffed
squeezed	pointed	puffed	aimed
kissed	called	needed	fussed
splashed	wished	preached	hatched
shouted	boxed	baked	marched
smoked	sniffed	huffed	planned
played	crashed	tripped	buzzed
stitched	nagged	rolled	hissed
sneezed	whipped	balked	wicked

52

Review

digging
smoked
married
trailed
Betty
licking
fibbing
stacked
hopping
penny
sniffed
puppies
setting
jelly
liked
boiled
skipped
bedding
stepped
matted

scrappy
sobbing
patched
fished
soaked
liking
hurries
stopped
played
letting
buggy
dizzy
slammed
wheeled
sitting
empty
filled
striped
sagging
happiest

blessed
clipping
chilly
scuffed
carry
witty
kitty
silliest
happily
shortly
muddy
wiped
candies
planned
quitting
nutty
stirring
badly
scraping
lazily

pinned
running
begging
varies
seated
trimming
whipping
sixty
needed
hoping
stories
rubbing
furry
greeted
Sally
spinning
budding
stretched
scratched
buggies

53

er   le

better	sickle	rocker	bangle
hobble	fumble	snuggle	tangle
mangle	riddle	summer	jungle
rubber	slipper	fiddle	cuddle
cobbler	winner	dinner	grumble
candle	muddle	dresser	ankle
able	tumbler	glimmer	blacker
settle	jingle	needle	single
saddle	uncle	platter	fizzle
peddler	prattle	trigger	supper
shopper	drummer	pepper	drizzle
helper	farmer	handle	ladle
upper	bottle	meddle	letter
angle	cripple	rubber	stopper
sizzle	humble	skipper	kettle
dipper	jumper	apple	crackle
snicker	juggler	puzzle	cattle
ladder	clatter	hammer	printer
Bible	bigger	guzzle	brittle
simple	tackle	flicker	table

54

Review

trigger	shouted	spotted	meddling
Peggy	sunnier	Bible	uncle
noodles	staring	dresser	angling
growled	riddle	ankle	gladly
sledding	follower	drumming	fishy
rugged	dropper	boxer	kicking
jumped	hungrily	parking	puzzles
padded	candies	fitting	whittle
bitter	tested	luckier	stamped
puffy	glimmer	puppies	pointer
tackles	buzzer	tables	splashy
matched	preacher	dipping	winners
berries	lining	trapper	sadder
called	shutters	thundering	betting
robed	crashing	fussy	dreamy
happily	bunnies	crippling	kisses
drizzly	baby	supper	kindly
sickly	snapped	missing	sizzle
crackers	reaching	handy	sandy
rubbing	aided	speedily	fiddler

55

pack—pace		truck—truce	peak—peace
	lack—lace—lacy	slick—slice—slicing	
place	pounce	bouncing	danced
prince	cell	cinch	Grace
since	fencing	Bruce	circus
forced	race	officer	traced
pencil	cent	choice	city
cigar	mercy	circle	space
notice	concert	ace	mice
mincing	face	icing	service
chance	cinder	braces	Nancy
glanced	groceries	fancy	parcel
spruce	rice	center	voice
citizen	cider	twice	France
advice	ounces	fancy	peace
dances	lacy	pounced	mince
faces	glance	cell	princess
ounce	fences	Alice	ace
mice	spaced	cinders	Bruce
raced	Francis	sliced	rice

56

rag—rage	bug—budging		dog—dodge
hug—huge	egg—edge		smug—smudgy
fudge	grudge	strange	passage
gentleman	cabbage	charge	stingy
orange	damage	larger	German
danger	stage	ginger	bridge
manager	strangers	pledged	fringes
gadget	cage	engine	magic
fidgety	urgent	hedge	ridge
age	George	gypsy	wedge
pigeon	lodge	nudged	gently
package	wages	hinges	page
gym	ledge	midget	badge
change	sledge	garbage	tinge
forge	bulge	hedge	gentlemen
damaged	nudging	gem	germs
engineer	changing	wage	energy
stingy	urge	fudge	passage
charging	page	forge	Marge
huge	nudges	magic	Gene

57

Review

pencil	truce	page	midget
lodge	Gene	fudge	danger
stage	service	pledge	mincing
braces	gypsy	fringe	citizen
fancy	chance	gentle	cider
age	George	ice	edge
slice	office	package	pace
racing	change	peace	advice
bulge	space	notice	magic
Bruce	badge	Marge	wages
cigarette	cabbage	ginger	bouncing
bridge	passage	nudge	truce
manager	face	forge	grocer
ledge	gym	sledge	ridge
fidget	dancer	judge	circus
spice	cinch	Nancy	rice
ace	force	garbage	gadgets
voice	gentleman	strangest	singe
princess	center	Grace	grudge
laces	circle	choice	smudge

58

se, si, sy as in cheese, rising, rosy

the, thi as in other, bathing

pause	dose	rosy	vase
excuse	raise	ruse	brother
bother	rouse	cheese	rise
father	those	gather	wither
wise	because	fuse	soothing
lather	hose	amuse	please
closed	suppose	rose	poise
nose	noise	mother	choose
teething	loathe	tease	whether
daisy	noisy	seething	breathe
rather	bathe	other	praise
easy	these	rouse	pause
fuse	excuse	other	these
cheese	choose	rather	lather
noise	rise	father	bathe
tease	pansy	soothing	hose
noisy	supposing	wither	close
vase	loathe	poise	raise
brother	because	posy	rosy
teething	those	pleased	amusing

59

Review

pledge	bridge	lather	suppose
wise	closing	danger	dose
bother	chances	manager	braces
sledge	judge	rage	gem
mincing	easy	nudge	since
notice	cheese	spicy	circle
center	amuse	vase	whether
pause	excuse	peace	stage
germ	ledge	nose	damage
mice	cents	concert	breathe
twice	glances	France	pleased
cabbage	service	passage	wither
grace	ridge	those	vice
father	lacy	rice	seethe
grocers	stingy	teasing	bulging
stranger	fidgety	races	Gene
pencil	roses	ounce	charged
packages	mercy	icing	edgy
spaces	Germans	dancing	wedge
badge	forge	gypsy	officer

60

Silent b, g, k, t, w

knob	knife	gnat	doubt
wrong	answer	gnaw	written
crumb	write	castle	rustle
debt	thistle	wrench	gristle
limb	wrist	wring	sword
wrestle	gnome	numb	hustle
soften	known	often	knot
nestle	christen	listen	lamb
knee	hasten	gnash	wrest
jostle	knuckles	climb	whistle
wrap	kneel	wreck	wreath
dumb	knock	know	gnu
thumb	knelt	gnarled	bristles
wretch	comb	knew	knit
knack	wrote	bustle	fasten
plumber	knave	castle	wrong
wrong	hasten	knelt	wrap
answer	knack	gristle	knitting
rustle	kneel	written	debt
wretched	whistle	comb	thumb

61

Silent gh, h, l

folk	mighty	eighty	sleigh
sight	tight	high	bright
calf	calm	naughty	sigh
fight	though	slight	weigh
eight	brought	caught	yolk
hour	bought	John	slaughter
thigh	honest	fright	flight
might	ghost	palm	eighteen
daughter	straight	thought	plight
height	knight	ought	freight
school	sought	light	through
weight	half	Thomas	taught
right	fought	lightning	honor
straight	bright	fright	thought
flight	palm	caught	sought
light	slight	mighty	weight
yolk	eight	plight	height
weigh	neighbor	night	through
fight	tight	though	naughty
calm	hour	eighty	freight

62

ph gh as in rough

phrase	orphan	photo	tough
autograph	elephant	nephew	pamphlet
pharmacy	enough	prophet	hyphen
trophy	triumph	rough	phonograph
laughter	cough	Philip	telegraph
phone	laugh	alphabet	roughly
enough	laughing	hyphen	coughing
prophet	elephant	Phil	phoned
tough	alphabet	phrase	Ralph
phonograph	nephew	photograph	laughter
autograph	telegraph	pamphlet	orphan
triumph	enough	nephew	phonograph
prophet	pharmacy	laugh	triumph
telegraph	tough	photo	laughter
pamphlet	elephant	rough	phone
cough	hyphen	Philip	orphan
alphabet	enough	Ralph	tougher
nephew	autograph	prophet	roughly
phoned	phonograph	Phil	enough
photo	pamphlet	alphabet	elephant

63

Review

phone	straighten	wreck	plumber
often	daughter	hasten	gnu
wrestle	alphabet	wreath	tight
answers	coughs	eighteen	frightened
soften	wretched	highest	knack
palms	climber	knaves	laughing
knocking	knots	wrist	crumbs
through	knitting	wraps	knife
castle	enough	knew	fought
hyphen	bright	school	write
gnashing	caught	ghost	jostle
autograph	balm	fasten	right
half	light	Ralph	lightning
written	thigh	Johnny	hours
whistle	orphan	knights	nestle
slight	mighty	Philip	swords
christened	eight	gnarled	thistles
gristle	brought	wring	telegraph
calf	kneel	weight	bristles
night	sight	Thomas	honest

64

Review

prince	phonograph	magic	because
bathe	though	officer	huge
fencing	sleigh	wages	pamphlet
rosy	noisy	cigars	wrote
hose	calm	engine	bouncing
smudge	known	teething	gnat
Bruce	raise	spicy	prophet
hedge	fancy	spruce	choice
wrong	these	Alice	parcel
elephant	urgent	soothing	dodge
ace	ought	knob	comb
sought	citizen	praise	bought
fuses	wrest	lodge	limb
age	fudge	naughty	fight
dumbest	midnight	knuckles	Ralph
doubt	debt	face	rough
truce	numb	gentleman	laughter
fringes	gadget	circus	rather
gnomes	noise	taught	large
honor	weigh	George	ginger

65

ea as in break, head, and learn

wear	pearl	instead	earth
dead	sweater	swear	weather
learn	ready	heard	breath
breakfast	steak	health	feather
bread	death	sweat	steady
head	wealthy	break	pear
bread	meant	tread	wealth
search	heavy	tear	spread
heaven	deaf	great	leather
bear	thread	breath	learn
heard	great	wealthy	sweater
breaks	bread	pearl	meant
search	head	healthy	feather
dreaded	treads	death	heavier
threads	earth	tear	steak
wear	wealth	leather	spreading
breakfast	heaven	swears	weather
ready	deaf	bears	heard
sweat	pears	steady	instead
dead	bear	health	steak

66

field	believe	siege	helpful
juice	fierce	full	butcher
belief	bullet	niece	careful
pull	chief	pussy	awful
thieves	shriek	pudding	bush
brownie	cushion	wasteful	cheerful
suit	grateful	grief	bull
bashful	priest	push	thief
fiend	yield	piece	pier
Charlie	nuisance	fruitful	brownie
full	awful	pudding	piece
pull	bruise	thief	juicy
pushing	suit	grief	believes
put	bull	wasteful	fruitful
niece	shrieked	fiend	helpfully
pussy	Charlie	butcher	belief
thieves	bullet	careful	brief
siege	fierce	cheerful	bashful
bush	priest	handful	pierce
shield	yield	fruit	grateful

67

water	wash	squash	trouble
enormous	jealous	word	war
country	touch	cousin	wander
watch	serious	quality	swamp
worse	couple	generous	nervous
marvelous	gorgeous	warning	what
double	worms	worst	worry
want	warm	world	dangerous
famous	worth	young	warden
curious	swan	quantity	work
worship	water	warn	world
marvelous	famous	courage	nervous
serious	quality	war	want
jealous	reward	generous	worship
worm	wandering	dangerous	couples
worries	worse	younger	cousins
squash	watchful	swan	warmer
gorgeous	worker	enormous	touchy
double	words	trouble	swamp
washing	what	worst	curious

68

Review

pierce	field	bread	quarter
thieves	priest	georgeous	worth
worse	ready	yield	swan
dangerous	thread	instead	marvelous
spreading	brief	couple	break
worst	Charlie	want	deaf
touches	heavy	dead	wealthy
brownie	what	pier	great
curious	pieces	learned	belief
bears	gratefully	steady	leather
nervous	dreadful	squander	shrieks
thief	handful	death	juice
wars	siege	cousin	squash
awkward	worship	weather	heaven
watery	quality	young	wandering
troubles	fruitful	butcher	double
swear	cheerfully	swamp	careful
jealous	enormous	putting	fruit
awful	heard	world	warned
nieces	suit	pudding	country

69

ci, si, ti as in special, pension, vision, station, action

su as in treasure   tu as in nature

station	measure	question	gracious
delicious	future	cautious	nation
social	attention	education	mixture
fiction	expression	permission	occasion
picture	action	treasure	vacation
pleasure	mansion	mention	nature
television	fraction	natural	special
usual	suspicious	anxious	vicious
pension	addition	precious	patient
social	precious	station	action
treasure	nation	patient	question
attention	mixture	measure	special
education	suspicious	gracious	delicious
mentioned	anxious	pleasure	future
occasion	fractions	pictures	cautious
natural	vacations	expression	permission
fiction	mansion	vicious	addition
nature	usual	television	exception

70

ive as in active   or   ance   ence   come   some

actor	passive	welcome	lonesome
traitor	handsome	someone	expensive
active	residence	razor	visitor
influence	become	native	conductor
captive	elevator	janitor	coming
favor	positive	flavor	providence
detective	instructor	tiresome	appearance
something	confidence	attentive	importance
income	performance	preference	sometimes
somehow	tailor	doctor	sailor
providence	motor	performance	sometimes
detective	visitor	passive	captive
influence	favor	welcome	coming
someone	razor	instructor	lonesome
somehow	doctor	residence	elevator
sailor	preference	handsome	importance
confidence	positive	conductor	native
appearance	actors	janitor	income
attentive	tiresome	expensive	flavor
traitor	active	become	something

71

Review

breath	preference	tiresome	residence
native	cushion	something	fraction
shield	providence	visitors	earth
patience	active	gracious	somehow
greatness	traitor	tread	fully
naturally	lonesome	pushing	watches
positively	vacations	permission	razor
future	performance	confidence	chief
importance	auction	sometimes	usually
wealthy	delicious	janitor	pleasures
attention	flavors	bull	Charlie
nuisance	station	mentioned	expensive
pulling	questions	treasury	tear
bruises	handsomely	mansion	expressions
vision	grief	vicious	motor
meant	healthy	sweating	addition
sweaters	pension	pearls	warning
doctor	anxious	passive	steak
generous	wasteful	mixture	casual
measured	outcome	fixtures	featured

72

Three-Syllable and Four-Syllable Words

innocence	difficulty	ordinary	underneath
exclaiming	Washington	quizzical	emergency
butterfly	passengers	jealousy	family
correction	Valentine	medicine	banisters
selfishly	exchanging	impatience	emperor
refreshments	thunderstorm	practical	banana
vinegar	Cinderella	exciting	mysterious
entertain	fashionable	impossible	threatening
attractive	peevishly	together	wonderful
amazing	committee	permanent	tomorrow
January	surrounded	lecturer	accident
beginning	favorite	December	earnestly
conversation	merchandise	perfection	decision
awkwardly	surprising	invitation	vanilla
newspaper	gorilla	suddenly	miserable
musician	unhappiness	American	holiday
restaurant	president	Mississippi	afternoon
transportation	dictionary	asparagus	understand
Thanksgiving	Elizabeth	secretary	February
liberty	independence	blueberries	democracy

Set in Linotype Baskerville
Format by Robert Cheney
Manufactured by The Haddon Craftsmen, Inc.
Published by HARPER & BROTHERS, *New York*